SERGE SAUNERON

Translated by Ann Morrissett

The Priests of Ancient Egypt

GROVE PRESS, INC.
NEW YORK

First Black Cat Edition 1980
First Printing 1980
ISBN: 0-394-17410-0
Grove Press ISBN: 0-8021-4276-1
Library of Congress Catalog Card Number: 59-10792

LIBRARY OF CONGRESS CATALOGING IN PUBLICATION DATA

Sauneron, Serge.
    The priests of ancient Egypt.

    Translation of Les prêtres de l'ancienne Égypte.
    1.   Priests, Egyptian.   I.   Title.
[BL2443.S283 1979]   299'.3'1   59-10792
ISBN 0-394-17410-0

Manufactured in the United States of America

Distributed by Random House, Inc., New York

GROVE PRESS, INC., 196 West Houston Street, New York, N.Y. 10014

The Priests of Ancient Egypt
by Serge Sauneron

Contents

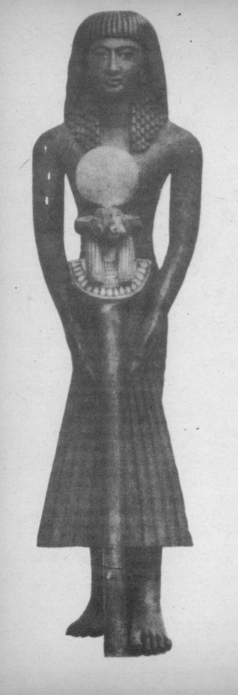

There are two outstanding features of ancient Egypt, both of which are strikingly evident on the banks of the Nile. First, its *art*, as the Cairo Museum reveals, is as old as history and as beautiful and perfect in its way as all that Greece and more recent civilizations have been able to produce in their greatest periods. Second, one sees that Egypt's monuments are nearly all products of religious preoccupations. From the plateau of Gizeh to the boulders of the cataract, in the shade of the Memphis palms and in the scorching inferno of the Valleys of Kings, in the calm of the Elephantine and in the white feluccas,[1] there is the same striking evidence at each monument, on each visit to the pyramids, temples, tombs, that everything constructed 'for eternity' – everything which has successfully by-passed the centuries – was conceived for the worship of the gods and for the immortality of man.

In no country, perhaps, has the desire for eternity been more eloquent, never more effectively realized. Houses, towns, palaces, all the architecture destined for daily life was essentially provisory: crude brick was sufficient. Thus little remains of these

---

1. Boats.

ancient towns. But beyond this world in which the living could express their joy in open air, beyond the created forms which are each evening eaten by the shadows, each morning given a new life, the domain of the unknowable remained ever perceptible. Outside of earthly time, in another world – in space but not precisely located – the gods and the dead triumphed over the dark forces predating creation, and lived forever in the joy of ageless youth. For these divine forces and timeless beings, there had to be houses which were as durable as the earth which held them: pyramids and temples are as immutable as the mountains from which their stone is taken, and underground tombs become part of the eternal rock which shelters them.

One becomes accustomed to seeing, in the ancient Egyptians, 'the most scrupulously religious of all men.' But this statement does not suffice to offer the keys to the Pharaonic civilization; in fact it would be a great error to consider the Egyptians too close to ourselves.

Nothing, without doubt, is more modern than these stone heads found in the mastabas,[1] than the bust of Queen Nofretete; nothing more alive, human in a reassuring fashion, than the scenes of daily life pictured in the tombs of Saqqara or of Thebes; nothing perhaps so directly familiar as the popular stories from the shores of the Nile. But beware of thinking that the ancient Egyptian was a man like us, that his civilization was basically analogous to ours, that his thinking was, in the progress of a world still imperfectly known, the beginning of modern thought.

To understand ancient Egypt, we must abandon the idea of finding in it our own culture and our own trends: we must accept this exclusion, and not delude ourselves with the apparent similarities. The Egyptian lived in a world very different from ours, astonishingly advanced in certain technical ways – in architecture, stone and metal work, works of art, moral thought – but also astonishingly primitive in the essential structure of his mental life, in his complete inaptitude for abstract thought, in his naive belief in a world created for man and made to his measure.

We like to talk about 'Mediterranean civilization' and include in it all that is beautiful or great in the vicinity of this sea. But when the Nile empties its seven mouths into the sea, it leaves far behind it everything that is distinctively Egyptian. For

---

1. Structures serving as entrances to the tombs.

Phoenicia, Carthage, Greece, or Rome, the Mediterranean is a means of connection, of human rapport, of commercial exchanges, of conquests; the common center of a world which can see itself from one shore to the other. But for Egypt, the sea marks the limit of a world – of an *African* world; thus the dreams of Ogotommeli, or the 'Bantu philosophy,' carry precious elements which help us to understand better certain aspects of Egyptian religious thought – but we must expect to find little of Platonic thought in this world.

To seek in Egyptian civilization a first version, still imperfect, of Greco-Latin humanism is thus a fruitless quest. One must, on the contrary, understand that a form of humanism totally independent of ours, produced by a society without any immediate connection with ours, has been able to create works equal to those which different needs have brought forth in our society.

If we can renounce modern man's pride and consent for a time not to compare the temple of Luxor to a cathedral, the Pharaoh to the current head of a monarchy, a royal sepulchre to the tomb of Napoleon; if we can admit that the divine beings worshiped in Egypt have little in common with the gods of Olympus, of the elegiacs and of Ronsard, and have even less to do with the god of the Jews, of the Christians, or of the Moslems, we will have some chance of understanding what constituted the Egyptian 'religion.' We will no longer be astonished to see the tombs exalt the forces of life, the divine appearing in everything which is capable of movement or of action. We can, in wandering through the temples, understand all that a perfect but precarious universe sought through vigilance and care to conserve its original stability. . . .

There are many ways of penetrating into the intimate lives of the ancient Egyptians, each way revealing some aspect of their daily life, some customary trait, some episode of their national history. If we try to revive the old Pharaohs, we will turn one by one the glorious pages of the past, some of them unhappy ones, but we will reconstruct only the official framework of Egyptian life. If we try to describe the innumerable lives of the little people, artisans of the villages and peasants of the fields, we will only succeed in elaborating an erratically documented history of the social and economic conditions of the country without having ever reached the individual lives of these men of long ago. If we go to the scribes, to the recorders of Pharaonic Egypt, many aspects of the intellectual, administrative, and social life will appear to us with a great luxury of detail, and the picture emerging from it will be both colorful and truthful.

In choosing for guides the priests of ancient Egypt, however, we hope to lead the reader into a world which is even more characteristic: that of religious thought and life. Political regimes, social conditions, economic factors are profoundly modified in the course of centuries; but at least one aspect of ancient Egypt remains constant: the attachment, during more than three thousand years, of these people to their religious beliefs, and the general scheme according to which they defined the relationship of man to the universe and to the forces which rule it. Our inquiry, then, seeks to answer several questions which are born inevitably from a survey of Egypt: why these temples and these tombs? Why these numberless reliefs, these statues carved from hardest stone? Why, on each wall, on each stela, on each object, these thousands of hieroglyphics? What men lived in these temples, and what were their thoughts?

LEAFING THROUGH OLD TEXTS

What visitor wandering through the museums never pauses, at least for a few moments, before the wonderful statues of priests which have disclosed to us the greatest periods of Egyptian art? The technical perfection of the work, the beauty of the material – breccia,[1] dark slate, gray granite – indicate the exceptional quality of the work. But what is the provoking riddle of the faces? What thoughts are hidden behind these serene features, what sights have been seen by these great, open eyes no longer animated by an inner spirit?

Leafing through the texts quickly, there appear several laudatory inscriptions: 'He was discreet about what he saw, a wise man, dressed in his habit, well-liked by his fellow citizens; a man whose coming was remarked, truly appreciated by his town, praised by his father, pampered by his mother, well-liked by his brothers. . . .' And these kind words are repeated from pedestal to pedestal, from statue to statue, varying sometimes in their terms, exalting such and such aspect of the life of the deceased, always enlightening, endlessly associating social qualities with the highest spiritual preoccupations.

Something of the ancient life is thus revived under our eyes:

---

1. A rock composed of angular fragments cemented together.

these cold figures, holding lovingly against them the statue of their god, become beings of flesh and blood; the vaguely smiling serenity of the faces seems to explain the indulgence of a soul entirely turned toward problems of the beyond, constantly listening for divine precepts. . . . We still seem to hear the ancient Greek writer describe with admiration the priests of the banks of the Nile:

Through contemplation, they arrive at respect, at security of the soul and at compassion; through reflection, at knowledge; and through the two, at the practice of the esoteric and dignified customs of former times. For to be always in contact with divine knowledge and inspiration excludes greed, represses the passions and stimulates the vitality of the intellect. They practice simplicity in living and in dress, temperance, austerity, justice and non-attachment. . . . Their gait is measured, their gaze modest and steady, without wandering to every side; their laughter is rare and does not go beyond a smile, their hands are always hidden under their habit. . . . As to wine, some never take any, others take very little, for they say wine harms the veins, and in confusing the head prevents speculation. [Porphyrius, *On Abstenance*, IV, 6-8.]

The impression received from the statues and the testimony of Porphyrius seem to concur in giving us a picture of the Egyptian priest which does not lack appeal: considering the technical wonders of the Valley of the Nile, its temples, its pyramids, its tombs; considering the evidence of a religious faith which appears in almost every object drawn from the Egyptian sand, one can pleasantly evoke a class of superior men, devoted to theological knowledge and meditation, from whom the subjects of the old Pharaohs found the inspiration for their art and the orientation of their lives. . . . Is it not logical to seek, in the life and culture of the priests of the Nile, the essential ideas which inspired such an important part of what today remains extant of the ancient kingdoms?

In looking through the old chronicles, in deciphering at random the stelae [1] and the religious monuments, in rereading the tales of Greek and Latin voyagers who, twenty centuries before us, were also tourists in Egypt, we will attempt to slip alongside these priests, still mysterious to us. Discreet but attentive, our

---

1. Stela: a pillar bearing an inscription, usually religious references.

thought goes out to study them, then to follow them, a little like the soul of the ancient Egyptians which came in the form of a bird to linger close to these once-familiar beings. . . .

The sage Petosiris will be our first companion.

THE EDIFYING LIFE OF PETOSIRIS

There is, in Middle Egypt, next to Mellaoui, a very old town once consecrated to the god Thoth: Hermopolis the Great. An immense mass of excavations, of brick walls, some Pharaonic constructions partly inundated, a beautiful Roman basilica and marketplace, are the most accessible remains. Somewhere under the row of palms is the most sacred place, the first mound which emerged from the initial chaos, from the creation of the world, and on which the first egg hatched, source of all earthly life. . . .

It is there that the sage Petosiris lived, during the last years of 'free' Egypt – a little before the arrival of Alexander the Great (around 350-330 B.C.). He was a very great personage in his town, bearing the most esteemed titles: 'High priest, seeing the Lord in his naos,[1] supporting his master, following his master, entering into the holy of holies, exercising the priestly functions in the company of the great prophets, prophet (himself) of six primary gods, chief of the Sekhmet priests, chief of the third and fourth class priests, royal scribe responsible for all the goods of the temple of Hermopolis, etc. . . .'

His life unrolls piously, occupied with serving the god, with restoring the sacred edifices in his name, with giving everyone an example of a pure and dignified existence. At his death, he was buried in the desert of Hermopolis, in the midst of waves of white sand, near the frolicing cynocephalus and white ibis, the sacred animals of the god Thoth. . . .

One day in the winter of 1919 his tomb was rediscovered; it had been conceived in the image of a temple, and its walls were covered with an astonishing number of reliefs and inscriptions. Some writings of Greek tourists, dating from the third and second centuries B.C., show how the great priest of Thoth was still celebrated, and how the fame of his virtues had gone beyond the limits of the city. 'I call on Petosiris,' says one of these, 'whose body is under the earth, but whose soul resides with the gods: sage, he is reunited with the sages.'

The inscriptions on his tomb impart a series of texts of philo-

---

1. The enclosed part of a temple, or inner sanctum.

sophical and religious inspiration astonishingly close – as much in the ideas they express as in the terms they employ – to the Proverbs of the Bible, and to the Psalms. Somewhat in the manner of the ancient books of Egyptian wisdom, those of Ptahhotep or Ani, certain inscriptions from the tomb of Petosiris, regrouped, furnish a sort of 'Collection of Maxims' intended for the living and extolling the favors and advantages which are found in this life and after death by those who 'live in the fear of the Lord and walk in His path.' We cannot do better than to cite together these four essential inscriptions as they have been grouped by the scholar who found this tomb and authoritatively published the texts, M. G. Lefebre:

> He who walks in thy path, he will not falter: since I have been on earth and until this day, when I have come to the perfect regions, there has been found no fault in me. . . .
> Oh you living. . . if you listen to my words, if you heed them, you will find their worth. It is good, the path of the one who is faithful to the Lord; he is blessed whose heart turns toward this path. I will tell you what befell me, I will teach you the will of the Lord, I will make you enter into the knowledge of his spirit.

Tomb of Petosiris

If I have come here to the city of eternity, it is because I have done good on earth, and that my heart has rejoiced in the path of the Lord, from my infancy to this day. Every night the spirit of God was in my soul, and at dawn I did as he willed. I practiced justice, I detested evil. I had no dealings with those who ignored the spirit of the Lord. . . . I did all this thinking that I would come to God after my death, and because I knew that the day would come when the Lords of Justice would make the final division, on the day of Judgment. . . .

Oh you living, I will have you know the will of the Lord. I will guide you to the path of life, the good path of those who obey God: happy is he whose heart leads him toward it. He whose heart is firm in the path of the Lord, secure is his existence on earth. He who has in his soul a great fear of the Lord, great is his happiness on earth.

It is useful to walk in the path of the Lord, great are the advantages reserved for him who follows it. He will raise a monument to himself on earth, he who follows in the path of the Lord. He who holds to the path of the Lord, he will pass all his life in joy, richer than all his peers. He grows old in his own city, he is a man respected in name, all his members are young as an infant's. His children are numerous and looked upon as first in the city; his sons succeed him from generation to generation. . . . He comes finally to the city of the dead, joyfully, finely embalmed by Anubis, and the children of his children live on in his place. . . . You have walked in the path of your master Thoth; thus, after having received the favors he grants you on earth, he will please you with like favors after your death.

Certainly these are very fine texts, and the one who conceived them had arrived at a remarkable spiritual life. But his city, Hermopolis the Great, was not, in the middle of the fourth century, among the most important cities of Egypt; the clerical circle was very limited, and the sanctuaries were in disrepair. The material framework of his education, the proximity of spiritual colleges whose instruction would have stimulated him, is not sufficient to explain completely the scope of his faith and the rigor of his moral life. Indeed it is remarkable to see *personal* religious fervor lead a priest to such spiritual summits above and beyond the normal priestly tradition.

Unhappily such was not always the case: we must recognize that Petosiris — and a few other priestly personalities whose lives we will recount – stand out from a rather dull background. Often, in fact, we only know the Egyptian priests by their names and the list of their titles, but we know nothing about how they really lived and how much piety appeared in their actions. Sometimes, going through the chronicles and archives on papyrus, we even discover a form of priestly life very different from the one we would imagine, picturesque no doubt, but lamentable. If one considers that the majority of Egyptian priests were honorable officials, convinced of the importance of their task and anxious to acquit themselves with conscience and fervor, and if it appears to us that this priestly body sometimes contained saints, it is necessary to recognize that it did not lack, on occasion, some unsavory characters.

One must not lose sight of the conditions under which the Egyptian clergy was recruited. From the old families, traditionally attached to the religion of their village, came, generation after generation, the new priests loyal to their faith, filled with the dignity of their function and the sanctity of divine service.

But all the religious offices were not filled in this way: sometimes it sufficed to be a functionary in the good graces of the sovereign in order to receive an important post in some distant temple: of what worth then were the practical knowledge and the fervor of the new priest? On the other hand, there were times when a well-filled purse was sufficient to buy a priestly office, and to enjoy, without too much trouble, a comfortable pension. Finally and above all, we should not forget that the priests were in office only during a limited time, three months a year perhaps, due to the alternations of those in service. In the course of each trimester which separated each month of actual service, their purely civil life flowed along far removed from the altar. In what way did the priests distinguish themselves, then, from the other inhabitants of their village?

The several extracts from the following histories have not been collected to destroy the noble idea we could be tempted to hold about the Egyptian priests. They ought only to put us on guard against a too-hasty generalization: the Egyptian priest-

hood was a function too *civil,* as well as too open, for us not to find all aspects of a society reflected in them, good and bad. On the other hand the priests were not the guardians of a divine mission for the faithful, but the simple executors of a daily religious ceremony which was performed far from the eyes of the profane. We will see that it called for very little preliminary training to be admitted into the ranks of the 'purified.' This lack of selection explains certain astonishing episodes in the priestly chronicles.

THE SCANDAL OF THE ELEPHANTINE

Let us transport ourselves to the south of Egypt, in the vicinity of the cataract. A modern town, Aswan, has succeeded the ancient settlements where the treasures of Africa used to arrive. In the west rock formations are the tombs of the princes of the Middle Kingdom. Toward the south can be seen the dam; beyond that the isle of Philae, like a water flower, takes its annual bath.[1] In the granite mountain, the ancient quarries from which came obelisks and statues. In the middle of the Nile, a miniature island, still bearing some ruins, a charming village

1. Since the building of the dam this ancient island is seasonally flooded.

and a *saqieh*[1] which grinds in the shadows of the palms. On this enchanting isle, where the feluccas loiter complacently, there was once a temple of the god Khnum, the great Ram of the cataract, guardian of the subterranean reservoirs from which the floods rush at the proper moment. It is there that we will reopen a judiciary dossier 3,000 years old, for this peaceful sanctuary was, under Rameses IV and Rameses V (1165-1150 B.C.), witness to a number of dramas.

The circumstances? They could be summed up simply: everything was going badly. Egypt had known great prosperity under the last of the great kings, Rameses II, several decades earlier. But the old sovereign was dead, victim no doubt of the intrigues of his harem!. . . . After that, the country got along as best it could in the hands of kings without real power – in the hands above all of every ambitious rascal who saw in the national chaos an opportunity for fruitful business.

Aswan vegetated gently: for a long time the rich Nubian caravans had not been seen passing, all loaded with gold and ivory from the southern countries, once so picturesque, glittering with their barbaric goods and ostrich plumes, their black porters bedizened with gold, and the bizarre animals – apes, giraffes,

1. Egyptian: water-wheel.

17

cheetahs – which they brought from the African forests as a gift to the Pharaoh. . . . Commerce was on its last legs, and the little markettown slept. By contrast, the temple of Khnum was prosperous, having been enriched some years earlier by the generosity of the kings. . . .

It is in this peaceful but deteriorating situation that several not very scrupulous individuals undertook to find greater resources. They were priests of the temple of Khnum, actively following the exploits of their leader, Penanouqi, together with a boatman of the area, whom they had won over to violent methods. These curious colleagues bought the authorities, the scribes, and the prefect with a part of their booty, and briefly terrorized the city with the notoriety of their crimes. Nevertheless they were, some time afterwards, put on trial, and it is in the judiciary document drawn up on this occasion that we have found the details of their exploits. Here are a few features.

The action began in the immediate vicinity of the temple; Penanouqi, the chief of the band, decided that the sacred animals lacked any utility at the moment; so he sold them, for a good price, to some priests and military personnel in the neighborhood. Then, on a voyage to Thebes, he became mixed up in a melancholy hoax concerning the oracle of the god, which no doubt gave him some mortification; to console himself, he seduced two married female citizens.

All this could still pass for diversion, but now he hurried on to more serious business. The temple contained riches of all kinds, the sterile presence of which, quite as much as that of the cattle, was a continuous torture for Penanouqi; so he promptly found a cure for his suffering. He appropriated a costly amulet in this temple, as well as the contents of a precious casket, and stripped the treasury of its goods. This done, as all the clergy undoubtedly were not satisfied, he agreed with his accomplices to modify the personnel of the temple and introduce some priests more open to the true problems. He maltreated a few protestants, cut off the ears of one, gouged the eyes of another, appropriating, in passing, twenty oxen destined for the temple, and, no doubt to keep up his good humor, set several buildings on fire. . . .

The other priests, meanwhile, unaware of this resourceful caprice which constituted the secret charm of their leader, but endowed on their part with a solid practical spirit, got their hands on the treasure of the goddess Anouqis. The scribe of the temple, who then acted as prefect, started to become angry, but a substantial percentage of the 'benefits' soon reconciled him. In the face of so much understanding in official circles, the priests, to console themselves for what they had to give over to their protector, broke the seals of the god's treasure, and without ceremony took sacks of wheat, lengths of cloth, garments, and other provisions, for which they promptly found use.

These memorable exploits did not continue, however, without repercussions. In particular the victims of these costly caprices made their protests heard in high places. An inquiry was begun, of which there are records preserved. What was the outcome of the trial? The text unfortunately does not tell us; but certain inscriptions written on the rocks of the first cataract, in the following years, show that some of the priests mentioned in the trial – and no doubt implicated by it – did not have, for all this, a less brilliant career. . . .

Thus the sole occupation of the Egyptian priests was not always prayer and meditation. How far we are from the fine words of Porphyrius and from the fine impression we received in reading on the pedestals of the statues of the priests the accounts of their saintly lives! . . . Let us still preserve some doubts on this untoward aspect of the priestly life as the enlightening history of the family of Peteisis lifts our last uncertainties.

THE MISFORTUNES OF PETEISIS

Around the year 512 B.C., a certain Peteisis, descendent of a once-powerful priestly family, was led to write the story of the strife which put his ancestors, for nearly 150 years, in opposition to the priests of a provincial cult of the god Amon. It is a story extraordinarily long and complex, but, briefly, here are the major facts.

The family of Peteisis, originally connected with the Theban priesthood, moved to a little market town in Middle Egypt, Teudjoi (today: El Hibeh), where they built a sanctuary to the god Amon; this occurred under the reign of the king Pasmetik I (663–609 B.C.). The family had lived there with priestly benefits accruing to their official charge, to which its legitimate proprietor, a high Heracleopolitan functionary, had ceded the family the right.

From this came all their misfortunes. In Egypt there was always a distinction between two kinds of benefits, according to which the office which justified them was the property of the

19

one who occupied it, or else it was a simple provisory charge conferred temporarily by the sovereign. In the first case, the benefits belonged as a right to the one who exercised such and such an office; he could then dispose of it at will, sell it, or transmit it to his heirs. In the second case, the benefits remained tied to the function, and changed proprietors each time a new incumbent took charge. However, Peteisis and his descendants never ceased to claim as their own the right to the benefits which were in reality the property of the high Heracleopolitan functionary – who was evidently illegitimate. But the priests of Amon, his rivals, had no more right than Peteisis; if they were authorized to withdraw Peteisis' privileges in order to restore them to their real owner, the high personage of Heracleopolis, they were at the same time infinitely less authorized to appropriate the priestly revenue which Peteisis possessed in his own right, and thus had the right to keep.

This conflict forms the plot of the long affair. But the account of Peteisis would be only a series of juridical chicaneries with no immediate interest for us, if there were not, mixed in with the story of the procedure, a living chronicle of the reactions of each of the parties at every step in this interminable quarrel. These episodes singularly enlighten us concerning the practices of the priestly life in the provinces. Here are some critical moments of this war between families; beginning with the opening of hostilities. . . .

Peteisis had legitimately enjoyed the benefits of his charge ceded to him by his proprietor, the high Heracleopolitan functionary. Up to this point, there was nothing to censure. But when in his turn he disposed of it in favor of his son-in-law Horoudja – rather than keep it himself, or return it to his benefactor – the priests decided to get rid of this intruder, and to divide among themselves the parts thus recovered:

When, in the morning, the priests gathered together at the temple for the division of grain among the classes of priests, the two sons of Horoudja appeared saying: 'Come on, let the fifth be measured.' [1] At this moment, the young priests drew out their sticks, surrounded the sons of Horoudja and began to beat them. The two young sons fled to the sanctuary, but they were followed there, and alas! caught in the very entrance of the sanctuary of

1. Evidently this refers to the fact that, as explained in the next chapter, there were usually four main priesty classes.

20

Amon, they were killed by the force of the blows. The priests threw their bodies into an interior section of the temple.

Neithemhat, the mother of the two victims, barricaded herself in her home; Horoudja, the father, carried a complaint to the police and called on his father-in-law for help. But 'when he arrived, he found no one.' This is still the case in Upper Egypt during the vendettas between rival families; everyone takes to the woods and disappears once the blow is struck, and the police arrive too late in a deserted village. . . . The priests, it appears, hardly concerned themselves with principles, and did not hesitate to use expeditious solutions. One can guess that the affair did not rest at that. Peteisis reacted vigorously, then pardoned the wrongdoers — for love of his town and to prevent an irremediable departure, but perhaps also because he was not unaware that the positions taken by him were arbitrary. . . . Thus the years passed, in minor skirmishes, the priests of Amon continuing to want to regain for themselves the benefits of Peteisis — settled by 'offering'(!) a part of them to their official owner, and the Peteisis family persisting in reclaiming hereditary possession.

But here in their turn the priests are victims of the appetite of a high personage, the superintendent of cultivated lands, who confiscates a part of their property. To regain their 'rights,' they buy the protection of a man in the good graces of the court, and find nothing better to offer him, to pay for his intercession, than an office of a prophet in the service of Essemtaouy, a descendent of Peteisis. . . . Foreseeing the pressures which would be exerted against him to make him give the man over, Essemtaouy fled from Teudjoi. Desperate, seeing their plans foiled, the priests felt only rage, and appealed once again, in a forceful manner:

> The following day they went to the house of Essemtaouy, seizing everything belonging to him, ransacking his house and the apartments of the temple; they had a mason come to tear down the stela which Peteisis had had placed in the temple. Then, from there, they went to the two stone statues, one at the entrance of the chapel of Amon, the other in the temple of Osiris, at the entrance of this chapel, and threw them in the Nile.

Exiled, his house destroyed, and knowing what all-powerful influences the priests had become in ingratiating themselves at court, Essemtaouy and his son Peteisis (third of the name) kept calm for a while. What good to protest? Peteisis had in vain sought to find himself a protector, the priests were untouchable, and he ended by allowing a compromise, returning to settle at Teudjoi, but not recovering the priestly benefits which had been stolen from him.

Third scene: Peteisis is requested, around this time, to write the history of these quarrels with the clergy of Amon, and to describe the responsibility that the priests had had in the fall of Teudjoi. Knowing wisely what awaits him if he throws any light on this sordid history, he flounders, refuses to talk, then finally, under the threat of the governor, he draws up a long report. The reaction of the priests was not delayed: reprisals would begin on Peteisis' return to Teudjoi. . . .

> When the new administrator learned what happened, he ran to the temple with his brothers armed with their sticks and falling on us, they beat us almost to death. Then they stopped and carried us to an old tower near the door of the temple, where they threw us with the intention of overturning the ruins of the tower on us.

This time again the old Peteisis escapes – beaten to the point where he had to spend three months in the hands of doctors. . . . His complaints obtain only a limited audience, his petition is long-drawn-out. Finally, the priests are beaten and released; returning home, believing he would find peace in this surrender, our hero passes neighbors who give him the bad news: 'Are you really Peteisis, who returns to Teudjoi? Useless to go on, your house has been burned. . . .'

The final complaints, the last punitive expedition to Teudjoi; the priests, in their usual manner, disappear, and Peteisis, defeated, discontented, downcast, reenters his town, without having been able to obtain either damages or guarantee of return. What happened after this we do not know; the papyrus stops at this point in the history.

Concerning the rest we are sufficiently enlightened; whatever the juridical background of the affair and the illegitimate character of the vindications of Peteisis and his family, the behavior of the priests of Amon was surely not exemplary: theft of priestly benefits, corruption of functionaries, intrigues, fraud – on occasion violence and murder – a rich balance sheet which gives us a curious idea of the ecclesiastical life at certain untoward periods of Egyptian history. What about religion, during these village brawls? What became of their god when

22

all the priests fled to the countryside for fear of the police? It is preferable not to dwell on this.

One can not avoid the idea that the priestly life, for many of these provincial priests, had been chiefly a way of having an assured income guaranteeing them a material livelihood, carrying only a few formal obligations, without moral commitment of any sort. Did they appreciate the importance of their office? One can only say the story of Peteisis is so strangely sinister that we no longer know if we ought to lend credence to the rare professions of faith which appear in passages of this long account: 'As true as your breath prospers, there are very great gods at Teudjoi; the great god Amon of Thebes comes into the temple, and numerous are the miracles that I have known there!' In view of the infamy of the actual proceedings, any quest for a spiritual life seems a grotesque paradox. . . .

After these stories, occasionally picturesque, if scandalous, it is high time to find a little purer air. Because of its lay character and the ever recurring 'rotation' in the life of the priest, the Egyptian clergy was evidently open to committing abuses of every sort. We have cited some to show the human part – too human – of the religious poses of the priests. We are going to see, nevertheless, that they were themselves aware of the dangers which threatened their moral life, and that they counted very much on the spiritual ideal of their office to overcome the temptations to which they found themselves exposed.

There are a few texts from the temple of Edfu which are a grateful contrast. Later we will have occasion to see all the complexity of the religion daily celebrated in this great sanctuary; it is conceivable that indifference at times caused the officiants to cut their service short, not to follow them to the letter, or to tolerate some irregularity in the hour at which the sacred rites were observed. These abuses the priests were called on to avoid: a number of fine addresses to the clergy of Edfu, inscribed on the doorposts by which the officiants of the sacrificial processions passed every day, in full view, urge them to the most scrupulous exactitude in the exercise of the religious rites, to a strict observance of the prescriptions of purity, and also to patience: some priests must have been tempted to deduct their part of the divine offering before the god had time to be satiated, evidently not without some danger to the universal order.

Oh you prophets, great and pure priests, guardians of the secret, priests pure in the Lord, all you who enter in the presence of the gods, masters of the temple ceremonies! Oh all you judges, administrators of the land, stewards in your month of service... turn your gaze toward this dwelling in which His Divine Majesty has placed you! When he sails to heaven, he looks here below: and he is satisfied as long as you observe the law! Present yourself not in a state of sin! Enter not in a state of impurity! Speak no lies in his dwelling place! Hold back no supplies, collect no taxes injuring the small in favor of the mighty! Add not to weights and measures, but make them smaller! Do no plundering with the bushel-measure.... Reveal nothing that you see in any secret matter of the sanctuaries! Lay hands on nothing in his dwelling, and go not to the heavenly flight carrying in your heart a sacrilegious thought! One lives on the provisions of the gods, but one calls provision that which leaves the altar after the Lord has been satisfied! See how he sails to heaven where he surveys the other world, his eyes remaining [fixed] on his blessings wherever they may be. [Edfu III, 360^{12}-362^5, transl. M. Alliot.]

One can see the temptations were so varied that the priests had only an embarrassment of choices. But it could happen that even a religious person, strict and rigorous during his month of service, relaxed once he returned to his normal life in the 'rotation.' It is partly to these priests on leave that the text gives this advice:

Countenance no falsity against truth in invoking the Lord! You who are men of importance, never let a long time pass without an invocation to Him, when you are away from Him present offerings to Him and praise Him in His temple.... Frequent not the abode of women, do nothing that is not done here; open no vessel inside the domain: it is the Lord alone who drinks there! Do no sacred service at your whim! What good then would it be to look at the old texts: the ritual of the temple is in your hands, it is the work of your children.... [Edfu III 361-362^4, transl. M. Alliot.]

In spite of the exactness of the terms, it is not inevitable that each prohibition applies to a crime actually being committed.... At least, it was considered possible, which is already eloquent. A last document, of greater significance, comes to conclude this series of texts borrowed from the great sanctuary of the

25

god of Edfu. It no longer speaks of misdeeds to avoid, nor of the vigilance with which the god surveys his prophets. It puts, on the contrary, value on the benefits of the spiritual life, the endless happiness of one who serves his god with a pure heart and a diligent spirit:

How happy is he who celebrates Thy Majesty, oh great God, and who never ceases to serve Thy temple! He who extols Thy power, who exalts Thy grandeur, who fills his heart with Thee. . . . He who follows Thy path, comes to Thy watering-place, he who is concerned for Thy Majesty's designs! He who worships Thy spirit with the reverence due the gods, and who says Thy office. . . . He who conducts the service regularly and the service of the holy days without error. . . . You who tread the path of Re in His temple; who watch over his dwelling place [occupied] to conduct His holy days, to present His offerings, without cease: enter in peace, leave in peace, go in happiness! For life is in His hand, peace is in His grasp, all good things are with Him: there is food for the one who remains at His table; there is nourishment for the one who eats of His offerings! There is no misfortune nor evil for the one who lives on His benefits; there is no damnation for the one who serves Him; for His care reaches to heaven and His security to the earth: His protection is greater than that of all the gods. [Edfu V, 343^{13}-344^3, transl. M. Alliot.]

The tone here is infinitely more serene – and the thought more elevated; there is no longer a question of reviewing prohibited offenses, but of exalting the virtues of an existence spent in the regular worship of the god, and the happiness that results from it. To two thousand years of error, the Ptolemaic texts of Edfu in the same spirit add their rejoinder, in the old exhortation of the book of wisdom of Merikare [ca. 2050 B.C.].

Do the monthly office of priest, don white sandals, enter the temple, open the secret places, tread the holy of holies, and eat bread in the house of the Lord.

The ecclesiastical life was not always then a simple material service, compatible with any kind of spiritual attitude; it could admit its spiritual ideal, placed in the most fervent devotion to the divinity, and in the rigorous observance of the daily ceremonies. Life, happiness, security, were in the hands of the god which made a gift of these to the faithful.

If we believed it necessary to show what could be, on occasion, the wretchedness of the ecclesiastical life and the indignity of certain of its representatives, the texts of Edfu, the exhortations of Merikare, and the maxims of Petosiris make us see all the fervor, all the riches of the spiritual life of an appreciable part of the Egyptian clergy, which were the reason and moral framework of its existence.

To be objective, one must recognize that the Egyptian priesthood, too liberally open and above all subjected to a very anarchistic method of recruiting, could attract an appreciable number of the 'misplaced' or profiteers devoid of human worth: every human collective of any importance inevitably includes some such types. One must also admit that the majority of those in the service of the religion were honest and conscientious, without genius perhaps, but at least faithful to their task and no doubt convinced of its nobility. Finally, we have been able to see that some of the priests were moved by a magnificent and infectious fervor, conveying a noble idea of the spiritual life and the theological meditation which could be inspired within the shadows of the Egyptian temples.

Thus the statues in the museums have not actually misled us; their praiseworthy inscriptions – even if their monotonous repetition can arouse some scepticism – correspond nevertheless in large measure to an ideal of the spiritual and social life which seems to be shared by the representatives of the priestly class today. But we have at least perceived an unsuspected fact which will cause us to go further into the study of the Egyptian clergy: a 'priest' in the Valley of the Nile has very little in common with the man whom we now call by this name. After this rapid survey and these several anecdotal insights which have shown the injustice there would be in judging too quickly a human group which was infinitely more complex than one would be tempted to believe, we must then seek the reasons for this difference, and define what the priestly function was both in theory and in daily life.

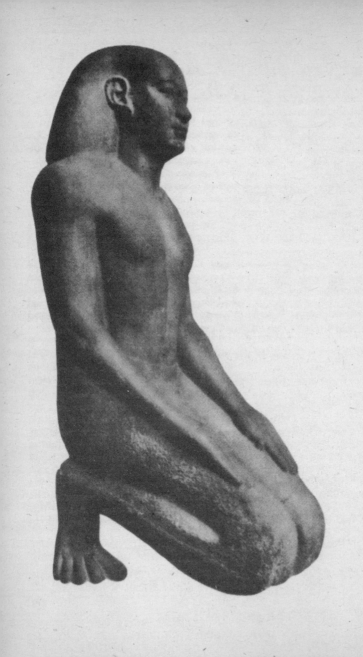

THE PRIESTLY FUNCTION

An unchanging country, its path always the same, a sun never hidden, a river which each year swells and overflows to give life to its banks: such is the framework in which the Egyptian spirit was formed, in which its main features took shape. Art, thought, the pattern of life, the mode of expression, everything in this country is initially marked by a static conception of things, unvarying in their eternal aspect or rhythm, as they were originally created.

In the first morning of the world, the gods caused the Egyptian land to be cast up from the primordial sea; they separated the firmament of the recovered earth, and hurled the sun up into the celestial ocean. Thus life was born – that of men, of animals and plants, of running things, of the earth itself, and its mountainous spines. . . . Everything was defined in the first instant, its name even determining its function; and in this world where nothing is accidental, the regular rhythm of the great cosmic or earthly phenomena – the day and the night, winter and summer, the ebb and flow of the waters, birth and death – impose the idea that the universe, predetermined since its creation, has been organized for all eternity according to patterns unvaryingly alike.

The balance of this world, the harmonious relationship of its elements, their necessary cohesion, indispensable to the preservation of established forms – it is this that the Egyptians call Maat. Maat is the aspect of the world that the gods have chosen, it is the universal order as they established it from its basic constituent elements, such as the course of the stars and the succession of days, down to the humblest of its manifestations: the harmony of the living, their religious piety; it is the cosmic balance, and the regular recurrence of the seasonal phenomena; it is also the respect for the earthly order set up by the gods – truth, and justice. The established world is thus an unchangeable form, determined in its phases as much as in its functions. But it is not a perfect balance, not a harmony unaffected by the defection of any of its elements. . . . As an infinitely complex mechanism each part of which would be granted liberty, this world could not survive; it could only maintain itself through

Pouring sand in the foundation trench
(Temple of Edfu)

The Scorpion King in the process of a foundation ritual

an unceasing control: the gods have need of a son who nourishes and protects their earthly spirit; these creatures call for a guide who assigns to each his role and his limits. This guarantor of the universal balance, this shepherd of men, is the Pharaoh.

THE ROYAL FUNCTION

No doubt the origin of this concept ought to be sought in the great silence of prehistory, in the times when the chief of the clan, embodying in himself the vital force of all his tribe, interpreter of the will of the god and agent for his action, was responsible for the material life of his subjects, all-powerful over the natural forces which he mastered by his unlimited magic power. It is from a social organization founded on a similar base that the religious and political structure of historic Egypt gradually evolved. Certain more powerful clans conquered or rallied the neighboring clans, formed themselves into little states, clashed in bitter battles for regional hegemony, ruled by turn, century after century. Then at the dawn of

history, the kings of the south, more fortunate than their predecessors, succeeded in making an organized state out of an anarchistic mosaic of clans. From this time, Egypt knew only one sovereign, master of the whole Valley, moral heir of the innumerable chiefs Egypt had once followed.

The master of the new state remained, however, in the superior rank which he had formerly had in his own little kingdom: the all-powerful despot, owner of the land and its resources, responsible for the swelling of the Nile, the rising of the sun, the birth of beings and of plants; the son of the gods, taking care of his forefathers and receiving from them in exchange the total power on earth to maintain the order determined by the gods. For this harmony to endure, it must be preserved on two levels: first, the propelling force must be maintained – the very existence of the gods, their divine activity in the world; thus the king would be responsible for religion. Then, the elements according to the predetermined plan must be maintained: to this end the legislative and judicial role of the king would correspond. 'To maintain the universal order, assuring the divine religion and giving its laws to men' – such would always be the double function basic to the king of Egypt, from the first of the Pharaohs to the last of the peasant Roman emperors, for nearly 3500 years.

Nothing is more obvious, in fact, than to state the permanence of this precise conception of royal activities. The first royal monuments known, at the dawn of the third millenium, show the Pharaoh in both his warlike and constructive activities: with hoe in hand, he breaks ground for the trench of a foundation or places the staves for the orientation of a temple under construction. Some thousands of years later, if we wander into the rooms of the great temples of Esna or of Kom Ombo, we see the same scenes of foundation laying accomplished by Pharaohs named Autocrator Caesar, Severus, Caracalla, or Decius! From the distant forests of Pannonia and Germania where the changing favor of the legions carried them to the imperial purple, did these emperors from the ranks ever suspect that they would go on to be officially considered in the far reaches of their provinces as the ministers of the Egyptian rites?

Aren't the foundation ceremonies for a sacred building still placed among those official acts requiring the presence of a supreme authority – or his representative? The inauguration of an important monument rarely passes, even in our time, without

33

Sethi I making an offering (Abydos)

official presence, speech, and ceremonies. . . . But in fact *all* the acts of the religion are performed, theoretically, by the king. If we glance over a wall of the temple, where the offering scenes and the various rites are detailed in long sequences, we will in fact be startled to note the *total* absence of priests; the king is performing the religious acts.

Obviously this was only a fiction. If it were possible for a chief of a prehistoric clan to be at the same time captain, administrator, and pope, the king of Egypt could not consecrate his life to administering, in a thousand different parts of the land, the religion of the divinities. . . . Until the clan disappeared, in favor of a unified kingdom, the tribal chief, becoming Pharaoh, by the same stroke lost the possibility of being the actual leader of the rites. He remains this in title, he remains this in the relief figures; but in practice he delegates his powers to the specialists who from then on performed this task in his place. Thus the official existence of the clergy rests, at its base, on this notion which has never disappeared of a *delegation of the royal powers:* it is in the name and place of the reigning sovereign that the priests of Egypt daily and throughout the land maintain the practice of the divine religion.

FUNCTION OF THE CLERGY

Of the double royal function, religious and legislative, only the first is delegated to the priests. This immediately characterizes the limited, specialized role of their activities: they would have to perpetuate the religion of the gods through the various external ceremonies in the temples which assure this function, but they would have only an extremely restricted social and spiritual role. We ought above all to guard ourselves, in using the term *priests,* against considering them as the guardians of a revelation which would make them a sect apart, living on the edge of society and only venturing to convert the crowds by impassioned sermons to a richer or more active moral life.. . . No, the Egyptian priests have a very precise role to play, as substitutes for the king, officiating in title only: to maintain the integrity on earth of the divine presence, in the sanctuary of the temples where this presence has consented to dwell – and this is all. Their action contributes to the essential theological role of the Pharaonic monarchy: to maintain the universe in the form in which the gods have created it. It is a work of specialists, a task of technicians. Once the necessary material

34

acts are accomplished to obtain this result, what the priests think or do is fairly unimportant – at least in the rigorous view of the State; they have nothing of the Hebrew prophets, nothing of the Christian priests about them. These are men like any others, not profiting from any divine privilege, not having to win over the crowds, nor to convert the gentiles; 'functionaries' of a sort, they are delegated by the king to perform in his place certain material rites necessary to the general welfare. The personal religion of the people is not indebted to them, and the priests themselves can even be fertile thinkers or saintly men – but as a consequence of their individual tendencies, not as a necessary result of their professional activity.

THE DEMANDS OF PRIESTHOOD

If the priesthood did not strongly imply a moral obligation, or – as we shall see later – a special technical training, it evidently required in the priest called to attend the temple certain conditions of physical purity.

The sacred edifice has only a few points in common with what we now understand by the word temple: it is not the place where the faithful go to pray to their god, it is not a building where men gather to treat of spiritual questions, trusting that the divine spirit will deign to manifest itself in the course of the ceremony; nor is it the place where a sacred rite is performed, executed by a specialist before a gathered crowd. . . .

The Egyptian temple does not admit the crowd: from the entrance of the sanctuary, a series of doors more and more effectively protects the holy place from the dangers of the open air. The darkness deepens as, room by room, one penetrates the heart of the edifice; the floors go lower, the earth appears, and, with an apprehension which increases from moment to moment, the visitor finds himself before the entrance, carefully closed, of the chapel where the divine statue rests. . . . For the Egyptian temple is the one place on earth where the god, diffused throughout the world, has a statue in which each morning a little of his nonmaterial body consents to 'embody' itself. It is this sacred effigy that the priest contracts to maintain religiously, to clothe, to nourish, and above all to protect from the attacks of evil spirits, always alert for some perverse blow. . . .

Therefore the men who can enter the temple and live every day in the immediate vicinity of the fearful idol have first to satisfy certain elementary conditions of physical purity.

35

The royal baptism

Even the term which designates the most ordinary category of priests, *purified,* calls to mind the initial ablutions of all impurity which the officials had to make: 'twice a day they washed themselves in cold water, and twice every night' [Herodotus II, 37]. These purifications were performed in the sacred lakes near the temples; before doing their service, in the morning, the priests went down to the water and sprinkled themselves copiously. When there was no lake, a stone basin or bowl took its place.

To this 'rite' there is already attached a certain symbolism; the water is, in religious thought, the primordial element from which life came – it is also where the dying sun, at sunset, goes to take new energy to rejuvenate it on the morrow.... Thus certain reliefs show a purification scene in which the water which falls from the pitchers is replaced by a rain of little symbols of life: the morning ablution then endows the officials with a new life which permits them unfailingly to maintain their daily service.

Another form of material purification to which the priest had to submit himself before entering the holy place consisted of washing the mouth with a little natron diluted in water.

Another rigorous obligation of the priestly life was to remove every hair of the body and head. 'The priests shave the entire body every other day,' Herodotus tells us, 'so that no impure flea or vermin shall impede them in the practice of their religion'; the statues and the reliefs have habituated us to the sight of these men with perfectly smooth pates. It seems that this operation constituted a very strict obligation, so much so that a fine of 1000 drachmas in the last epoch was put on those who dispensed with this measure. Various texts state precisely that the priests must shave or depilitate themselves up to the eyelashes and the brows of their face.... It was an absolutely general measure, and we know for example that the Greek voyager Eudoxus of Cnidus, who did research among the Egyptian priests to initiate himself into new knowledge, was only admitted among them when he had shaved his head and eyebrows. [Diogene Laerce VIII, 8 (87), 3.]

Another custom attached to the pursuit of bodily cleanliness was circumcision: 'They were circumcised for cleanliness, for they put cleanliness above aesthetics. [Herodotus II, 37.] The candidates for the priesthood were not always circumcised, for one could enter the priestly apprenticeship at a very young age, but they probably submitted to this operation the moment they officially acceded to their charge. Under the emperor Hadrian, circumcision became a distinctive mark of the priests. In what measure had this practice previously been in current usage? Did it constitute, in the great epochs, one of the necessary conditions of the priesthood? We do not know enough to say so. At least the writers in the last epochs had some difficulty in finding theological causes. Hasn't Saint Ambrose explained, with the seriousness which only pertains to pure souls, that this witness of devotion to the sacred cause 'put to flight the prince of the demon?' [Ad Constantium, 72.]

To believe the Greek and Latin authors, the priests of Egypt had little occasion to appreciate the pleasures of the table; Herodotus, no doubt, pictures their menu as an attractive one [II, 37], but the voyagers who succeeded him do not agree. They inform us that the priests had to abstain from a little of everything: of slaughtered animals, sometimes, the head must be shunned, sometimes the feet, sometimes the anterior members [Origen]; they did not eat cow [Chaeremon], nor, with more reason, pork [Aristagoras de Milet; Flavius Josephus; Plutarch]; sheep were forbidden [Aristagoras], also pigeon [Chaeremon], pelican [Horapollon], and fish – above all seafish –; vegetables [Plutarch], beans [Herodotus II, 37], garlic [plutarch; Origen], all were held in horror; wine was to be drunk only in small quantities,when one did not completely abstain [Plutarch], and even salt, water-produced though it was, could not appear on the table [Aristagoras; Plutarch]. . . . Poor priests – especially since they were obliged, when young, to deprive themselves of the little consumable food that they were still allowed. . . .

But the truth seems to have been otherwise. It is likely that each of the animals or vegetables cited above was proscribed in some place in Egypt, but not all at the same time: the food prohibitions were in fact attached to the religion of the *nome*; in consequence of such misadventure as may have been reported by mythology, the god of each religious metropolis held in awe a given animal – more rarely a plant. It was the duty of the priests of the area to abstain from eating the meat – or the milk – of this forbidden animal; but this prohibition applied only to the clergy of the geographical zone of the religion in question. In one place, the sacred animal, which varied according to the god in favor, would be proscribed from the table, whereas the neighboring village would make it a part of their normal consumption. This was sometimes the source of contention between the small villages. 'In our time,' Plutarch recounts [Isis and Osiris, 72], 'the people of Oxyrrhinchus, because the people of Cynopolis had eaten of the oxyrrhinque [fish of the Nile], seized some dogs, killed and ate them as victims. From this came a war in which the two towns both suffered very much. In the end, this difference was regulated by the Romans who punished them.' An infallible way to be disagreeable to one's neighbors was evidently to put in a casserole the animal which they had made the earthly incarnation of their god. . . .

One can conceive, in this connection, that the priests were obligated, according to the place, to abstain more than anyone else from this or that food, following the religious obligations of the god that they served.

Let us say finally, in honor of the priestly class, that they did not lack companions who knew how to appreciate good cheer and bend the elbow: the priests of Coptos who honored Satni, or yet the celebrated Pcherenptah of Memphis, companion in pleasure of Ptolemy Auletus, were apparently men who knew how to live well. At least the latter had the spirit to inscribe the exhortation on the funerary stela of one of his wives: 'Oh brother and husband. . ., priest of Ptah, never cease drinking, eating, becoming intoxicated, making love, passing the time in merriment, following your heart day and night; never put chagrin in your heart: what are the years, as numerous as they may be, that one passes on earth? . . .' All that we know of him leads us to believe that these were superfluous encouragements. . . .

The priestly life indicates still another kind of physical purity: sexual abstinence, at least during the periods in the temple. The Egyptian priests married: their duties did not compel them to celibacy; at the most, if one can believe Diodorus [I, 80], they were supposed to content themselves with one wife, inasmuch as the people outside the temples had the leisure to enjoy several; but this restriction itself was not general, since the happy Pcherenptah, already mentioned, established a veritable harem. Their private lives seem to have varied considerably according to the individual. But at least they had to be pure when they passed through the sacred enclosure:

> The prohibition against uniting oneself with women in the sacred places or entering there after leaving the arms of a woman without washing oneself comes from Egypt [Herodotus: II, 64].
>
> Nearly all men, except the Egyptians and the Greeks, make love in the sacred places and pass from the arms of a woman into a sanctuary without washing themselves; for they think that men are of the same rank as beasts, and they see them, the earthly species as the winged race, making love in the temples and in the places consecrated to the gods; if this displeases the divinity, they conclude, the beasts would not be doing it either.

On this point the Egyptian texts are explicit: whoever goes into the temple must be purified of all feminine contact by an abstinence of several days.

By their exterior appearance, the priests were easily distinguished from other Egyptians. Certain cloth was forbidden them, above all wool, a material provided by living creatures, contaminating the one who wore it and offending the sanctity of the places called them. This prohibition seems to have been absolute: the unanimity of the authors who report it [Herodotus, Apulius] and the strong fines which were imposed on offenders attest to its imperative character.

The priestly habit had to be cloth of fine linen, and to correspond to one unvarying cut; in all epochs, in fact, the priests seem to have preserved the austere habit that they wore in the first days of Egyptian civilization: at most, a detail of their dress could indicate the exact function that they fulfilled, for example, the sash the reader-priest wore across his chest. The only ones who had the right to different dress were the specialized priests and the high priests: the *sem* priest, thus, would be garbed in a panther skin, whereas the high priest of Heliopolis would be draped in a skin constellated with stars, and the high priest of Memphis would have the right to a collar of special shape, and a side plait.

If one excepts the high personages of the cults, the priests were noticeable in the Egyptian crowd by the archaic sobriety of their costume; no doubt this archaic quality, in a society in which everything was considered good that suggested antiquity, was an important element of their prestige.

Let us add, finally, that the wearing of white sandals, among people who walked voluntarily in bare feet, appears to have been one of the privileges of the priestly class. At least the classic authors judged it thus, and the Egyptian texts put 'white sandals' among priestly privileges.

As strange as it may seem, there was almost never any question, in the appointment of priests, of theological knowledge. The correct performance of the religious acts indicated there was an apprenticeship; but it seems that many elements were taken into consideration in the choice of a new priest – except this one. Did the newcomers learn their calling through practice only, once they were introduced into the temple enclosures? This is what we would be led to believe if the existence of a remarkably developed sacred science, and the indication of theological meditation prevalent in the little world of the temples and sacred rooms, did not demonstrate that theological training was obligatory. But we are almost com-

pletely ignorant of its forms. At the most, we know from a very late papyrus that a candidate for the priesthood had to pass an examination on religious subjects [Pap. of Tebtunis II, 291]. But the earlier epochs are almost mute on this point.

ACCESSION TO THE PRIESTHOOD

It seems impossible to discover a general rule for all the Egyptian clergy – or for each epoch – defining the conditions for admission to the priesthood. It would seem that the relative simplicity of the priestly obligations ought to have opened the priesthood very widely to masses of candidates, but this was not the case; the priestly life implied duties, and also included considerable advantages, in a country where fear of the next day has always been the dominant sentiment of the masses. Thus religious office was the object of endless covetousness.

There were always certain threads appearing – or following concurrently: inherited rights, co-optation, the purchase of offices, all permitting a ready recruitment which was generally convenient. Responsible families, generation after generation of the same religion, could be sincerely attached to their god and show proof, in the exercise of their function, of a real fervor; in return, they would be certain to enjoy a lucrative post where they could also, as was sometimes the case, sleep in the shadow of the altars and do only what was strictly necessary to justify their presence.

Confronted with this conception, which had its defenders, one must not lose sight of the fact that the religions – whatever actual rights may have been acquired by the priestly families in the service of a god over the years – remained a *royal delegation,* the Pharaoh being practically the sole minister of the religions of Egypt. It was up to him, then, at any time it appeared opportune, to place whoever seemed appropriate to him in whatever position he wished; such a system, poorly defined in its principles, inevitably led to conflicts – which were never lacking. The story of the religions of Egypt is the permanent reflection of the unfortunate interferences of these multiplex systems. We will examine each of them successively.

INHERITED RIGHTS

'When a priest dies,' Herodotus tells us [II, 37] 'his son is put in his place.' In practice, this was evidently not the absolute rule, but it was at any rate a tradition solidly implanted. The Old Kingdom already gives us examples of testaments by which a priest bequeathed his function to an heir: he disposed of it like property. There are plentiful examples of functions – priestly or otherwise – left to a beneficiary with power to transmit from son to son, heir to heir. In the New Kingdom, it came about that a man could reclaim a priestly charge in a temple simply by saying that he was the son of a priest of the religion. Better still, the stelae of the Low Epoch occasionally reveal the geneology of those to whom they are dedicated, and some of them claim for themselves seventeen generations of ancestors who were priests of the same god: one can truly speak of priestly dynasties.

We must judge this state of things by the general tendencies in Egyptian society. Without doubt it was not as rigorously stratified as the Greek authors would like us to believe; it was not quite true that an infant, born in a given milieu, had no other course than to assume the profession of his father: there was a certain flexibility among the various trades. But if this inheritance of functions – or simply of trades – was not a law without repeal, it nevertheless constituted a very general tendency: the society showed a clear propensity to stabilize itself, to fix itself in a given course. Isn't one of the strongest wishes that an Egyptian could express, in his prayers to the gods, to see his son put in the place that he, the father, had occupied?

We can understand, under these conditions, how the provincial priestly families, to whom the responsibility of a religion had been entrusted, had come to consider that this honor and this advantage should remain in the family. But even with the passage of such a charge from father to son, legitimate as this 'inheritance' could appear, the idea of a royal favor remained: it is by the grace of the sovereign that the son is able to replace his father in this function. The king Psamtik (ca. 648 B.C.), to recompense Peteisis for services which had particularly satisfied him, gave him the title of priest in all the temples where his father had formerly exercised this function – and this, although Peteisis himself had never before been a priest. . . .

Thus, in the little towns of the provinces, the priestly families could usually see their functional charges remain in their hands: but as frequent as was the transmission of a priestly office from father to son, the hereditary character of the priesthood was never anything but a custom, the *right* always remaining with the sovereign to name whom he pleased where he pleased.

SELECTION AND PURCHASE

The royal whim could thus, at any moment, intervene in local arrangements, where the priests organized the composition of their clergy among themselves. In practice, royal interference was rare, simply by reason of the considerable number of temples and the astonishing number of priests: the priestly families could flourish without too much fear. When the 'laws' of inheritance did not suffice to fulfill the needs of a given cult, another procedure was put in operation, selection by the group.

The priests in office met together in a committee and agreed among themselves on the name of the fortunate one elected to join the holy ranks. . . . This practice was probably employed most frequently when it was a question of filling vacant posts. No doubt each new priest, even when he belonged to the family of one of the temple officials, had to be accepted by the priestly council and confirmed by the drawing up of a diploma.

Finally, the last periods of Egyptian history show the right of purchasing priestly offices, with all the revenues that these offices carried: the fee that one had to pay for this bore the name, in Greek, of *télestikon*. In the imperial epoch, this practice seems current, especially for the offices of stolist and prophet. But if we are certain of the occasional practice since the Middle Kingdom, we are less certain of the manner in which these purchases were made in the earlier periods.

THE ROYAL NOMINATION

Every cult, in whatever temple, was practiced in the name of the king: 'The gods have prepared the way for me: it is the king who sends me to contemplate the god,' says a chapter of the ritual. Each priest, in some way, had to be nominated by the sovereign. It is obvious that such a centralization would have required a considerable ministry and great delays. Thus in practice the king reserved to himself the nomination of the high dignitaries of the church, the highest pontiffs of the great cults, leaving to the Minister of State the nomination of priests of lesser rank.

When the young Tut-ankh-amon restored the clergies of Egypt, a period devastated by the turmoil of Armana, we learn that he 'installed prophets and priests chosen among the sons of local dignitaries, the children of prominent men whose names were known.' In this, the sovereign moved wisely, replenishing the temples in a way that satisfied provincial self-respect; it was a clever technique to reconcile the dignitaries who had been injured by the too personal authority of Akhenaten.

At other times, the king could promote a priest whose personality and service pleased him. This was the case with the priest Nebouay, in the time of Tuthmosis III, who was successively promoted to the rank of first prophet of Osiris, then, some years later, became, by royal favor, first spokesman in the temple of Ahmose I at Abydos.

45

Yet royal intervention had no other effect, here, than to legitimately recompense the services of an old churchman grown gray in office. It came about that the official promotions had a different purpose, especially when they bore on the nomination to a given post of a priest intentionally chosen from a different clergy. Thus Rameses II went to seek the first prophet of Amon among the dignitaries of a clergy in the Abydonian region – to the great injury, certainly, of the Theban priests who must have coveted the position. . . .

On his return to Thebes, Nebounnef was introduced into the Thinite nome and led before His Majesty. He was then first prophet of Onouris, first prophet of Hathor, queen of Dendereh, and chief of the prophets of all the gods in a given zone. Then His Majesty speaks: 'Thou art henceforth high priest of Amon: his treasuries and his granaries are under thy seal. Thou art the head of his temple, all his servants are under thy authority. As for the

Tut-ankh-amon

temple of Hathor, queen of Denderah, it will pass into the hands of thy son as well as the functions of thy father and the position that thou occupiest. As true as the god Re loves me and my father Amon praises me, I have appointed to him all the personnel of the court, the chief of the soldiers... the prophets of the gods and the dignitaries of his house, who behold his countenance: none satisfied him until I said thy name! Be then devoted to him, for he reclaims thee. . . .'

The courtiers, with an accomplished hypocrisy, celebrate the divine choice, carefully directed by Rameses, and the ceremony ends:

> And His Majesty gave to Nebounnef his two rings of gold and his sceptre of election; he was named high priest of Amon, head of the double house of silver and of gold, head of the double granary, chief of works, chief of all trades in Thebes. A royal messenger was sent to let all Egypt know that the house of Amon was turned over to him, as well as all its property and its people.

This technique seldom varied; we know from the stela of the high priest of Ptah Pcherenptah that 1200 years later the kings proceeded in the same way to nominate the supreme pontiff.

Therefore we can consider that *generally* the royal nomination intervened only in two specific cases: when the sovereign wanted to recompense a priest (or a dignitary) whose services he appreciated; and when, for reasons of internal politics, he wanted to modify the balance of forces by choosing the supreme pontiff of the Theban clergy outside the, already too powerful framework of the priesthood of Amon. Outside of these two conjunctures, it seems that the accession to various degrees of religious office was regulated by one of the three procedures cited earlier.

THE INSTALLATION

On this final phase of candidacy for the priesthood, we are unfortunately much less informed than we would like to be. The bilingual texts of the Ptolemaic epoch show that this ceremony involved a ritual, *the ritual of installation,* but its forms are not easy to determine.

To adhere to certain texts, it seems that after the purifications required of any person entering the temple, the new priest simply received a kind of summary baptism: 'They went to seek Ptah-

The King goes before the god ►
(Temple of Edfu)

nefer, the new prophet of Amon, led him to the temple and anointed his hands, in order to initiate him into the service of Amon [*The Tale of Peteisis*]. The procedures would have been identical with the introduction to nonpriestly offices: we *assume* an office, the Egyptians *anoint themselves* to an office.

But the text of a statue in the Cairo Museum gives us some supplementary details:

'I present myself before the god,' says a priest, 'being an excellent young man, brought to the edge of heaven. . . . I came from Noun (primordial waters) and I have rid myself of all that was evil in myself; I have set aside my clothing, and ointments such as those used by Horus and Seth. I come before the god in the holy of holies, full of fear in his presence.'

Presentation at the temple, purification, sight of the god, such then are the stages of this consecration. Evidently it carried with it certain advantages, the passing on of certain secrets that only the initiated priests could know – the communication perhaps of those magic formulas which permit the *enchantment of heaven, earth, hell, and the seas – to see the sun climb to heaven with its cycle of gods, the moon rise, the stars in their place* [Roman of Satni, cf. p. 122]. The temple was not simply a building – indifferent stage for the acts played there – but a miniature image of the world, a kind of model representing symbolically the regions of the universe where the god moved; this seems the evident explanation of the various symbols turned over to the young priest at the moment of his installation.

Let us remember in this regard the rites which marked the

initiation of Lucius into the cult of Isis in Rome, as reported to us by Apulius [Metamorphoses XI]: a priest who is his elder first reveals to him, according to the hieroglyphic scrolls, the rites which accompany his installation; then Lucius purifies himself *in the nearby pool,* and receives the *sprinkling of purifying water;* the priest then leads him *to the very feet of the goddess, and gives him in secret certain instructions which surpass the human word;* this is the preliminary phase. The priest candidate has to fast for ten days, and the same initiation occurs; far from profane eyes, one envisions Lucius in *a robe of linen which has never been worn, and the priest, taking his hand, leading him into the most secluded part of the sanctuary.* There he receives the final revelation which he evokes in these terms:

> I approached the limits of the dead; I trod the threshhold of Proserpine, and I was carried beyond all the elements; in the middle of the night I saw the sun shine with a brilliant light; I approached the gods from below and from on high, I saw them face to face and I worshipped them near at hand.

Scholarly interpretations of this celebrated text abound, showing that the young priest made a cosmic voyage, and died to our world to be reborn transformed. It seems incontestable that the 'mystery religions' had strongly influenced the spirit in which these initiations were conceived, and that numerous influences are manifest in them which owe more to Greek mysticism than to Egyptian traditions. It seems to us nevertheless – and the reader may judge, after the citations evoked at the beginning of the paragraph – that the phases of the ceremony, in their form if not in their spirit, came very close to what they might have been, around the same epoch, in the temples of Egypt.

Figure from the beyond
(shroud of second century mummy)

THE WORLD OF THE TEMPLES

Fortunately we have been able to escape the turbulent battalions of tourists; there they are flowing again toward the temple doors, where a long line of carriages awaits. For another few minutes yet the air will resound with cries and the cracks of whips, then calm will descend once more over this great world of ruins. . . .

We are at Karnak, at the top of the first pylon, in the evening of a warm day in winter. On one side, the Nile and the Theban mountain, somber now under a reddening sky. On the other side, the temple of the god Amon, immense and magnificent, with a harmony unexpected in this great chaos of stone. . . . As far as the distant walls, the monuments crowd together, superimpose themselves, surge up like plants, crumble in cascades: pylons, obelisks, statues, columns, rows of sphinxes, chapels, until out of sight. Somewhere to our right, we discern the sacred lake, and its calm surface lined with the flights of birds. . . . And outside the enclosures we sense other ruins, hidden behind palm trees, more temples, more lakes, more statues, and sphinxes.

This impression of grandeur we have already felt before: Dendereh, Medinet Habu, Philae, each in its own fashion, are astonishing worlds, a jumble of structures solidly implanted over an immense area: the great gods needed space, sanctuaries as vast as cities, where all the opulence of the capitals, the pomp of kings, the great monuments of history were translated into a language of stone. . . .

And while the dusk descends over the great enclosure – tinged with the blue mist of the villages – the attrition of the centuries disappears; the temple seems as it was at the height of its glory, when a crowd of believers enlivened its doorways. In the complicity of the night and of silence rediscovered, all the figures from the past engraved on the wall break from their prison and come to move among us. . . .

The first pylon of Karnak

For a whole world of priests populated the greatest of these sanctuaries; from the high priest, eminent political personage in the State, to the last chaplain or artisan, a throng of servants, priests, assistants of every sort and degree of competence filled all the courts and corridors of the sacred enclosure with their teeming life. At Karnak, when Amon was in favor, hundreds, perhaps thousands, of the temple personnel were present in the course of a day. Under Rameses III (1198–1166 B.C.), a papyrus gives us the total number of men in Amon's service – priests as well as peasants of the land, hunters, boatmen, administrators, diverse workers: a total of 81,322 people!. . . . And we learn from the same document that this privileged god had at his command 433 gardens, 924 square miles of fields, 83 boats, 46 construction yards, and 65 small market towns exclusively devoted to the upkeep of the holy domains. Seeing these figures, one understands the exceptional importance of the personnel of Amon and one can easily imagine the astonishing quantity of priests and men of every function who might be attached to the cult and to the material administration of such an organism. Up to 125 diverse functions can be counted among the personnel in the service of this all-powerful divinity.

This was evidently an exceptional case; compared to this colossal fortune, that of the other sanctuaries was singularly meager. Heliopolis and Memphis, for example, the two largest cities in the country after Thebes, had at their disposal resources infinitely more limited: a personnel corps equal, respectively, to $1/7$ and $1/27$ that of Amon; as to the rest, here is the comparative table of property of each of these three temples:

	Thebes	Heliopolis	Memphis
Men	81,322	12,963	3,079
Beasts	421,362	45,544	10,047
Gardens	433	64	5
Fields	924 sq. m.	170 sq. m.	11 sq. m.
Boats	83	3	2
Workyards	46	5	
Market towns	65	103	1

The overwhelming superiority of Thebes appears beyond

question. Yet Heliopolis and Memphis were very large cities. . . .
Contrasting with these all-powerful clergies – veritable states
within a State – we shall find in turn cults struggling along in
a confined area, forced to be satisfied with one or two officials
– even with gods who the texts tell us possessed no private
clergy, and who lived from the surplus of the richer gods who
were willing to receive them. . . .

Between these two extreme cases were the large majority of
the Egyptian temples with medium-sized clergies. Such a temple
as that of Anubis at Fayoum, near the pyramid of King Sesostris
II (1906–1888 B.C.), was ministered by fifty people: six permanent priests and four alternate groups of eleven part-time
officials. Elsewhere, in the city of Aswat, the god Oupouaout
contented himself with some ten servants while Teudjoi, the city
of Peteisis of whom we spoke in the first chapter, possessed a
clergy of eighty part-time priests – twenty a month – to which
probably a few permanent attendants should be added. We are
not likely to be greatly mistaken in concluding that an average
sanctuary had a permanent staff of from ten to twenty or
twenty-five ministers.

THE PRIESTLY CLASSES

Not everyone, of course, is a priest in this disparate crowd
which lives in the temple enclosure, but many are in one fashion
or another. By priest we must indeed understand every man
who, through bodily purification, puts himself in the state of
physical purity necessary to approach the holy place, or to touch
any objects or dishes of food consecrated to the god. The process
was brief and the installation, at least in the lower orders of the
priesthood, encountered hardly any delays, but it is certain that
if the number of the 'purified' was considerable, there remained
an abyss between the ordinary chaplain and the priest permitted
to see the god.

Therefore a certain number of priestly classes exists, among
which are the many temple guests having a right to be called
priests; one can also distinguish among the high clergy, the
low clergy, and the auxiliaries; but problems abound the moment
we try to define each of these classes more precisely.

In the first place, they are 'floating'; certain groups of the
cult figure now with the high clergy, and now with the lower –
the pastophores, for example, or even the singers; perhaps according to the needs of each place they were considered either

essential or secondary. Or perhaps their importance increased with time; we must in fact deduce the sacred hierarchy entirely from the Egyptian sources, numerous in every epoch, and from the Greek lists, which can but reflect a late view of the priestly organization.

Even these sources are insufficient, for various categories of priests or specialists functioning in the temples could not systematically be attached to one class or another: this is the case with the administrators, sometimes priests but most often laymen. It is also the case of the technicians: priest-readers, sacred scribes, timekeepers, who play a very important role in the religion or in the temple life, but can easily pass for specialized laymen. Therefore let us adopt a somewhat more detailed classification based on the role actually played by each attendant, rather than on the spiritual importance of his activity which varied considerably.

THE ADMINISTRATIVE PERSONNEL

When a temple was of modest proportions, possessing only a little land and maintaining only a small staff, the administration of it was simple. It confined itself on the one hand to verifying the regular harvesting of crops which furnished the table of the god and that of his ministers; on the other hand, to overseeing the religious services and the satisfactory progress of the ceremonies. There are any number of texts which show priests from small sanctuaries accumulating religious as well as administrative titles, and passing from divine service to counting sacks of wheat. . . .

When the temple began to take on some importance, this accumulation of titles became impossible. The temple of Amon at Thebes, for example, possessed its own administrative staff – a veritable ministry – in which the religious personnel took no part: directors of the domain, chief scribe of the domain, accounting clerks, military chiefs, recruiting chiefs holding important posts, along with the chief steward, the steward, the superintendent of personnel, and the police chief. . . . The collection of taxes was assigned to the chief of flocks, director of the horned, hooved, and feathered beasts; the fields were under the control of the director of fields – or of arable lands; the harvests were dependent on the chief of the two granaries, while the treasury was placed under the high authority of a treasury director, chief of all that is placed under the command of Amon.

Each of these high administrators had under his own command a whole army of lieutenants, scribes, and subalterns.

The same papyrus from which we have taken the list of possessions of the three great clergies of Egypt gives most eloquent figures as to the annual land rents from each of these temples: the clergy of Amon, for example, collected considerable weights

of gold, silver, and copper, clothing, sacks of grain, and fowl
by the hundreds of thousands. . . .

One imagines the number of scribes, the thousands of archive
papers, the offices of every description which such an organization required, and one can imagine why the priests placed
the responsibility for it on a special administration.

In practice, however, the various members of the temporal administration were not excluded from also being priests. The administrative body of a temple, with its temple director, its chief of herds, its treasurer, its scribe, its chief of the granaries . . . was frequently presided over by the prince of the *nome,* who also had a few priestly responsibilities. Hapidjefa, nomarch of Aswat in the time of Sesostris I [ca. 1950 B.C.], considered himself a member of the body of priests with the same status as the priests officiating in the temple.

In time, however, the duty of administrator progressively lost its clerical aspect; the *lesonis* of the low epochs (an office which had become *annual*) is much more a manager than a priest, and his replacement in the Greek and Roman periods, the *epistate,* actually became the *civil* chief of the inalienable religious property, having under his control the collectors who bring in monetary contributions, the stewards charged with overseeing the holy lands, and the accountants who keep the books up to date.

THE RELIGIOUS PERSONNEL

Included with this partially clerical administration is the personnel of the cult, under the name of 'servants of the god' — which the Greeks translate, somewhat loosely, as *prophets.* The Egyptian god is not, in fact, an abstract power which one can worship anywhere; he is an all-powerful lord, physically present in the holy sanctum. The attentions due him are for the most part material: food, bodily care, etc. This staff of priests can be compared to that which is occupied with the affairs of a lord in his castle also bearing the name 'servant.'

On many occasions we find the ordinary temples in the hands of simple 'servants of the god' limited in number. But as soon as the sanctuary took on some importance and its personnel became numerous, a hierarchy established itself among the various persons having a right to the same title. As is logical, the innumerable clergy of Amon was the most divided and subdivided: one can count up to four classes of 'servants' possessing a hierarchical standing, and a fifth class of simple 'servants' not yet integrated into the *cursus* of superior grades. This division of prophets by class extended from the clergy of Amon, where it was indispensable, to a few other clergies whose abundant personnel justified a similar division.

It would seem to us logical, once this hierarchical sequence was defined, to see the priestly careers progress regularly according to the successive stages of the religious functions. In fact, we have knowledge of numerous documents showing that one passed readily enough from the inferior or intermediary degrees, and that the *cursus honorum* was less rigorous than one might believe at first glance. At least one can assert that 'advancement' followed a progressive selection, and that the number of priests called to succeed to the highest grades was reduced the higher they rose in the hierarchy.

Thus, in the Theban priesthood of Amon, the *second prophet* was already unique in his rank, and occupied a privileged place in the State. He was a very great personage. . . . Occasionally he replaced his superior, the first prophet, as his numerous functions, political as well as religious, frequently took him from the temple; but above all he had the upper hand in an important part of the 'temporal power' of Amon, the overseeing of the workers in the fields, and the control of the outside contributions to the god. A whole household might find itself placed at his service, and a whole army of functionaries, of scribes, of direct subordinates, who prepared the administrative documents in his name, and assured the smooth running of the services placed under his control.

As for the *first prophet* of the god, the 'high priest,' he was a very eminent personage, whose power in the State was evidently linked to that of the god he served. He sometimes carried a special name, related to the exact function that he assumed originally in the religion of his god. Thus, if the high Theban pontiff simply called himself *first prophet of Amon in Thebes,* the one in Heliopolis carried, if one believes a recent interpretation, the eloquent name of *he who is able to see the Great (God),* a title which became, reinterpreted by the following generations, *the great one with visions of the god Re.* As for the high priest of the god Ptah at Memphis, he carried the technical title of *great chief of the artisans,* all industry being, we know, placed under the eminent patronage of the god Ptah.

The first pontiffs could sometimes rise from the ranks, having climbed (or scaled) the various levels of the priestly function. In the important clergies of the country, it is much more usual to see the fate of the high priests depend on the political climate and on royal favor. They could be chosen from among all the prophets of the house of Amon, all the personnel of the court, and the high generals of the army; but the king was free to choose outside these favored categories: this was the case with Nebounnef. This liberty of choice permitted the sovereign to put new men devoted to him at the head of the ecclesiastical states and to resist to a certain extent the ever-increasing demands of a too-powerful clergy: we shall see that very often the supreme function was bestowed by the members of these clergies, who had become the highest personages of the State. Once the high priest was named by the king – and especially when he had been chosen outside the clergy that he came to head – it was the custom to confirm his nomination by an oracle of the god; politically and divinely installed, the new pontiff then received two gold rings and a symbolic staff, as the king pronounced the traditional phrase: 'Thou art hereby made high priest of the god X: his treasuries and his granaries are under thy sanction, and thou art chief of his temple.'

Such were the elements of the superior clergy of the gods of Egypt, the class of 'servants of the god' who could, following the hallowed expression, 'open the doors of heaven' and thus daily contemplate the god of their religion. They formed the priestly elite, the ecclesiastical group in which the highest dignitaries of the Egyptian clergy were included, sometimes even the sovereign pontiff of the great religions.

Along with this privileged class there was the innumerable mass of *low clergy,* and of the auxiliaries; but we must first imagine a world somewhat apart from the priests – those who entered only into certain specific acts of the religion, whom we shall call *the specialists.*

THE SPECIALISTS

These technicians are generally numbered, in the lists, among the superior priests or in the rank of subalterns; no doubt they were sometimes among one, sometimes among the other – and sometimes outside the two categories. In fact, it is more the specialized character of their function which interests us than the spiritual evaluation which made them either high priests or lowly auxiliaries.

Among these priests destined for the specialized offices were first of all the *stolists,* well known from Greek documents: these were the officiants who, every day, had to care for the body, the clothing, and the ornamentation of the divine statues and to maintain in appropriate rooms of the temple the jewels, clothing, and other objects of the cult. These stolists did not have, so far as one can judge, any special designation in the hieroglyphic texts: the documents of the Middle Kingdom speak of a *chendjouty*, 'the priest of the private clothing,' who is perhaps a stolist; but when the inscriptions of the late epochs want to describe these priests, they have recourse to a long paraphrase explaining that these were *the men entrusted to the personal care of the god, who enter into the holy of holies to ornament the gods with their material belongings* [Decree of Canope]. This is to say that this role originally had to go to one of the 'servants of the god' who held only this title, in spite of the specific privileges that he received. Later, they judged it opportune to give a special designation to the ministers who dressed the divine statues.

Among the number of specialists the scholars and intellectuals of the House of Life should be included. We will later have occasion to study in detail what we know of these suprareligious institutions; let us say simply that these were the rooms near the temple where the liturgical books necessary to the cult were written, among others, and where the elements of the sacred body of knowledge were worked out. To these institutions were attached the scribes of the House of Life, the scholars, the personnel of the House of Life, those the Greeks called *hierogrammats*. Certain of them were priests, especially esteemed; the rest, because of their vast culture, were official representatives of wisdom in the temple enclosure. It is among these that the clergy-representatives for the king were, on occasion, chosen, when official missions required the participation of the sanctuaries of Egypt. Thus, in the year 4 of Psamtik II (591 B.C.), when a priest had to be found to carry the gift of Amon to the king, they chose, at Teudjoi, Peteisis, scribe of the House of Life, a literate man of whom one could ask anything one wished, sure to obtain from him a satisfactory reply. The renown of this wisdom crossed the sea, and numerous passages in the Greek and Latin texts speak of the wisdom and the technical knowledge of the sacred scribes: they could heal the sick [Horapollon I, 38], knew the medicinal plants [Galien], geography [Herodotus II, 28], the signs of the sacred animals, the history of the ancient kings [Diodorus], knew how to foretell the future [Josephus, Suidas, Elien], and even how to make rain fall [Ammien Marcellin]. . . .

Their colleagues the priest-readers, scribes of the divine books, baptized *pterophores* by the Greeks because of the great feathers which adorned their coiffures, share with them this universal renown and popularity in their own country. These knowledgeable scribes were not always priests: there is often mention of them in a purely lay context; for example, they voluntarily occupied themselves with medicine and many papyrus medical prescriptions are attributed to their knowledge [Medical Papyrus of London 8, 12 and Med. Pap. of Berlin 8, 10]. In the funeral ceremonies, they participated as private ritualists, performing the beatific ceremonies to the blessed spirits according to the secret books drawn from the wisdom of the priest-reader. Finally and above all, they represented for the Egyptian people the same type of popular magician, hero of romances and fables, that have become part of our folklore. Thus the prophecies that the king Snefrou was pleased to hear, in the earliest period of the Old Kingdom, were attributed to the priest-reader Neferti, a scholar of the eastern delta; while the stories about Cheops tell us of the misadventures of the priest-reader Oubaoner who knew, through magic, how to get rid of a rival who pleased his wife too well. The same stories acquaint us also with the famous Djadjaemankh, a very clever sorceror whose tricks could restore his lost good humor to the sovereign. Finally, let us not forget that the popular story of the apprentice-sorceror grew out of a tale of Lucien, creating a sacred scribe of Memphis; here is how the spiritual author of the *Philopseudes* recounts the misadventures of Eucrates, his hero:

I was yet young, and I sojourned to Egypt where my father had sent me to complete my studies. One day I decided to go up the Nile to Coptos, and to see the statue of Memnon and hear the marvelous things that it renders to the rising sun. I heard it then, not like ordinary mortals, emit an inarticulate sound; but Memnon himself opened his mouth and spoke an oracle in seven verses, which I would recite if it were not inappropriate.

In going back on the river, it happened that there was among the passengers a citizen of Memphis, one of the sacred scribes, a man admirable for his knowledge and versed in every doctrine of the Egyptians. They even say that he spent twenty-three years in the subterranean sanctuaries where Isis taught him magic.

It is Pancrates of whom you speak, says Arignotos; he is my master, a holy man, clean-shaven, dressed in linen, pensive, speaking Greek (but badly), large, flat-nosed, prominent lips, spindly legs. . . .

It's the same man, Eucrates puts in, it's certainly Pancrates. . . . At first, I was unaware of who he was; but in seeing him, every time the boat dropped anchor, perform miracle on miracle, in particular riding the crocodiles, and swimming with the sea monsters, who bend down before him and caress him with their tails, I recognized that here was a holy man; and little by little, by courteous attention, I became his comrade and we became so intimate that he revealed to me all his secrets. In the end, he invited me to leave my servants at Memphis and follow him alone, telling me that we would have no lack of people to serve us. Since then, this is how we have been living.

When we arrived at the hostel, my man took the bolt from the door, or the broomstick, or the pestle, covered it with clothing, and pronouncing over it a magic formula, he made it walk, and everyone took it for a man; and the object went to fetch water, fixed our provisions, accommodated us, served us in everything with courtesy and ran our errands. Finally, when the magician no longer had need of his services, he made the broom a broom, or the pestle a pestle, by pronouncing over it another incantation. Eager as I was to learn his secret, I could not obtain it from him: he was jealous of it, although he put everything else entirely at my disposal. But one day, being in an obscure enough corner, I heard the incantation without his seeing me. It was a word of three syllables. He then went out, after having told the pestle what to do.

The next day, the magician being out to handle some affair, I took the pestle, dressed it like an Egyptian, pronounced the three syllables and ordered it to carry water. When it had filled the vase and brought it to me: 'That's enough,' I told him, 'don't carry any more water and become a pestle again.' But not wanting to obey me, he kept carrying more, so much and so well that by all his fetching he had inundated our house. I was very much embarrassed, for I greatly feared that Pancrates, on his return, would be angry at me, which in fact did happen. So I took a hatchet and cut the pestle in two; but each of the two pieces took up vases and went to get water, and in place of one water-carrier, I had two.

At that moment Pancrates came in; he understood what had happened and made the two water carriers back into the pieces of wood they had been before the enchantment; but he left me without my seeing him go, and disappeared I don't know where. . . .

To these specialists there were further attached two series of priests, the *horologues* (priest-timekeepers), and the astrologers. On the first, the most diverse opinions have been expressed, then vulgarized by the manuals in general use. One thought, for example, that these 'religious' ones were only in fact the right-thinking laymen who came each for an hour, to offer their services to the temples – benevolent gesture of a sort; this explanation of their quality permitted a justification of the numerous contexts in which they appear. In fact, it seems that the priests of the hour were quite another thing: the astronomers charged with establishing the hour and specifying, day and night, the moment in which each act of the cult should start. These are the ones which certain texts lead us to picture perched on the terrace of the temples, following with their eyes the progress of the nocturnal heavens.

As to astrologers, they had to know the mythological calendar and to explain to those who asked which were the feast days and which were days of mourning in the Egyptian year. In fact numerous calendars of this kind have been found, in which each day of the year is described as good, neutral, or bad, according to events of the divine legends which had taken place this same day in the past. Certain days were particularly overcast: whoever had the troublesome idea of being born on such a day inevitably had to die in such and such fashion. . . . When a son of the king was born, at least if we are to believe the popular tales, the fairies replaced him – the seven Hathor goddesses – so as to be sure of his fate. But one imagines that the noble ladies would not trouble themselves at every birth, and that the father, fortunate or unfortunate, had to go himself to inquire of the calendar specialist the favorable or unfavorable predictions; this was the role that the horoscope-priest had to fulfill. Later, in the last epochs of the Egyptian civilization, the horoscope-priest became even wiser: the idea had filtered into Egypt to tie the destiny of each individual to the cosmic circumstances of his birth: thence came the custom – for a brilliant future – to 'draw' from the horoscope of the newborn the astral influences which had been dominant at the hour he came into the world. But this practice, much later, was not connected with the early Egyptian sources. We can also consider that the horoscope-priest, if he existed permanently in the sanctuaries of the great epochs, had to content himself in defining the fortunate or unfortunate nature of birthdays, working from the mythological events that happened on these dates.

Equally specialists, the singers and musicians played an important role in the religious life of the temple. The cult in fact included not only the latter; in various moments of the service there were musical interludes sung with harp accompaniment. We will speak later of the musical serenade which woke the god in the morning; texts elsewhere, at Dendereh, and at Medamud, among others, are composed on a rhythmical theme with passages for chorus and for refrain. These arrangements required specialists.

We are amply informed concerning the musicians and sacred singers, both men and women. The importance of their role seems to have increased with time: Clement of Alexandria, for example, ranked the singers, the *hymnodes,* among the superior priests; he saw to it that the notes should be exact, that the rhythm of the melopias should conform to the old traditions of sacred performance; also that some exercise was necessary to train the artists, whose social status was superior. Under the Emperor Julien, at the very end of the pagan era, they again gathered at Alexandria sacred musicians for the religious ceremonies [Julien, *Letters,* 109 (56)].

In the oldest epochs, we are much less sure that the singers of the temples were great personages. An entire series of economic and social documents of great interest, the stelae of deeded gifts, show us enough poor fellows, proprietors of a little bit of land and fond of fine music – their own, at least – who gave themselves, body and goods, to a temple: in exchange for their artistic talents, the clergy had to assure them the security of a living; all of which leads us to think that the fiscal exactions and the military confiscations did not guarantee the same privileges to those in civil life. . . .

As to the feminine personnel, which we see here for the first time in the temple enclosures, they seem to have enjoyed a social situation very much more perceptible. In fact, it seems that on occasion the women had the possibility of exercising a priestly charge; since the Old Kingdom, the examples of priestesses and goddesses – and even of gods – are plentiful: women of high society – or simply daughters of priests having received the office of their fathers by inheritance – seem to have been able to perform the ceremony as well as men.

67

With time, however, this principle became dulled, and the specialization of the feminine role in the cult was increasingly encouraged: the Theban institution of an earthly wife of a god, the *female divine worshipper,* who occupied an eminent place in the clergy of Amon, remains an isolated case, without parallel in the other religious assemblies; but the presence of women singers or musicians in the temples is a little more usual: the reliefs frequently show them shaking their *sistra* [timbrels] or playing the zither before the god in order to please him with their harmony.

Outside this artistic role, the women seem still on certain occasions to be very limited: for example, in the representation of the religious mysteries, two young women played the role of the goddesses Isis and Nephthys: 'Let there be brought forth two young women pure of body, virgins, plucked of all hair, head ornamented with a wig, a tambourine in hand, with their name written on their shoulder: Isis, Nephthys; and let them sing the verses of this booklet before the god.' [Papyrus Brit. Mus., 10, 188.]

This scene, if one believes another papyrus [Berlin, 1425], was played before the portal of the propylaeum of the temple of Abydos. But we cannot state that the young people called to fill this office had been taken into the permanent personnel of the temple: like many other 'specialists,' they could be invited to play a role in religious ceremonies in an occasional capacity, after having simply satisfied certain conditions of puritiy. Such at least was the case of the two young girls, which the Greek texts have accustomed us to call 'the twins of the Serapeum.' Their story would be too long to report in detail, but here are at least the essential facts. Their mother had run off with a Greek soldier; their father, in fear of being killed by his rival, fled to Heracleopolis, where he died. The two young girls, left to their own devices, went to ask asylum of the priests of the Serapeum of Memphis, where there was a friend of their father [163-161 B.C.]. There, in exchange for the subsistence which was given them, they had to play the role of two sister goddesses, Isis and Nephthys, at the funeral ceremonies accompanying the burial of the Apis. Their lives would have flowed along thus in relative tranquility if new misfortunes had not come to trouble the stream. But that is already another story. . . .

We have had occasion to underline the fact that the priestly body attached to a given temple had at the same time a few

Stela of a musician of Amon

permanent priests, and an alternating series of officiants. This rotation was determined by the system of the priestly cults – which the Greeks called *phylai*. Here is its principle: the temporary personnel was divided into four groups, exactly parallel in number and in distribution of functions. Each of the groups carried out the religious service for one month; in other words, each priestly *phyle* actually 'worked' only three months a year, each of these periods being separated from the following by a three-month period of liberty. In the Ptolemaic epoch, a fifth *phyle* was created, reducing further the participation of each group in the maintenance and operations of the temples. Each of these four – or five – groups had at its head a tribal chief, the *phylarch*. At the end of each month of service, the departing *phyle* ceded its place to the one replacing it, and turned over to it the temple with its goods and problems: it was on this occasion that the temple inventories were made, on tablets of wood or sometimes papyrus, wherein the incumbent *phyle* could, at the moment it took over its duties, establish the presence of all the utensils and religious objects necessary in the temple: statues, musical instruments, portable chapels, ritual vases, etc. . . .

THE LOW CLERGY

Under the general term of 'low clergy' are ranged all the priests having right to the title of 'purified,' but enjoying in the cult and in the course of the sacred activities only a secondary role; these were, in brief, simply minor clerics.

These 'purified' could have the most diverse functions: porters of the sacred ship, charged with watering the temple, overseers of the painters and designers, chiefs of the scribes, artisan chiefs of the sacred domain, or simple artisans themselves, responsible, for example, for the sandals of the god. . . . In the temples of a more developed clergy, they were further divided into classes, certain ones being more 'purified' than the subordinate groups but without any particular description in the vast category of priests-of-all-work.

Among the members of the low clergy were the *pastophores,* bearers of sacred objects, of which the role – and even the name – again poses some problems not easily solved. The priests who slaughtered the sacrificial beasts were apparently not simple butchers: the Greek texts identify them as lower officiants, and certain Egyptian texts rank them among the personnel of the House of Life, showing that they had to know certain principles

Inventory tablet
(Temple of Maat at Karnak)

of religious symbolism, and that their function greatly surpassed a simple material act: the animals destined for the gods had to be selected and killed according to certain standards.

Finally, the *interpreter of dreams*, whom the Greeks call *oneirocrite*, was a scribe well instructed in the science of nocturnal apparitions, remaining at the disposition of the faithful who were curious to know the significance of their dreams; in the epochs where the custom had spread of spending the night in the temple to receive the advice of the god, it is presumed that the explanation of dreams became an important activity of the chaplains of the low clergy.

THE AUXILIARIES AND OCCASIONAL GUESTS

Finally we must mention the numerous personnel of auxiliary laymen whose activities permitted the material functioning of the temples, without their being, properly speaking, part of the world of priests: the doorkeepers and guardian beadles of the sacred buildings, the less important personnel of the shops bakers, butchers, florists, even their overseers, the offering-

Slaughter scene (Theban tomb)

bearers at whose long-syllabled intonations, twice a day, food is brought to the altars of the god; the sweeper, who erased all trace of footprints on the sand of the chapels; then all the squads of artists and architects, engravers, painters, sculptors, who repaired, constructed, decorated the religious buildings according to directions from the scribe of the House of Life, the hierodules with ever-uncertain functions; the personnel, finally, of assistants who looked after the sacred animals, providing them their pittance and, on occasion, showing them to tourists in return for a fair fee. . . .

Aside from these innumerable auxiliaries, who could only make modest claim to the priestly title, the temples received still another strange species of individual about whom we must say a few words. There were first of all the *voluntary recluses*. The increase, in the later Egyptian civilization, of pious civil institutions which kept themselves to a strict moral regime and contributed, by their generosity, to the upkeep of the sanctuaries, favored the existence, in the sacred enclosure, of civil groups who were making, shall we say, a kind of retreat; these pious people retained the privilege of leaving the temple when it suited them. On the other hand, another category of individuals found near the altars not rest

for the soul but a veritable *asylum* from the dangers of the outside world: police, tax-collector, conscription, and other evils; we can imagine this picturesque and miserable cortege of tattered beggars – or slashed bandits – who came to beg in the shelter of the inviolable walls of the sacred domain a morsel of bread and the assurance of escaping a sad end. Certain ones vowed themselves, apparently for life, to the service of the god, like the pious rabble of *catoques* of the Serapeum of Memphis, or the voluntary recluses of whom we have found evidence in several contracts: in exchange for some service they did for the priests, they obtained their protection against the world, and could exercise some accessory function in the service of the divinity: a certain, Tanebtynis, taking vows to the god of a little temple of Fayoum, dedicated himself with the following phrases:

> I am thy servant, as well as my children and my children's children; I can never go out of thy grounds; thou wilt keep me, and protect me, safe and sound, thou wilt defend me from all evil spirits, male or female, from all sleepwalkers, all epileptics, all nightmares, all the dead, all the drowned, all evil spirits. . . .

As to wrongdoers, they had to content themselves with the material security that the temple enclosure offered them, and discharge, in exchange, several petty jobs justifying the subsistence they received.

In addition to these voluntary refugees appear the sick, coming to seek relief for their ills or, by way of dreams, the recipe for their cure. And in the latest epochs the temples came to know an astonishing category of guests, the *visionaries* and the *fakirs:* the texts of the 'Astrologues' have left us lively portraits of these:

> The abandonment of all bodily care seemed a testimony to their spiritual perfection; half-nude, clothed in rags, they let their hair grow like horses' tails, and sometimes, as a symbol of their voluntary imprisonment, they weighed down their emaciated bodies with chains. No doubt they also imposed rigorous abstinence on themselves, and discipline, and their asceticism made them appear worthy, in the eyes of the common people, to receive divine revelations. [Fr. Cumont.]

74

Sometimes they explained to visitors, tourists and pilgrims, the divine legends, playing the part of dragoman; often they gave out oracles in a state of trance, thus deriving some benefit from the 'divine' madness which possessed them.

Chapel bearers (Temple of Denderah)

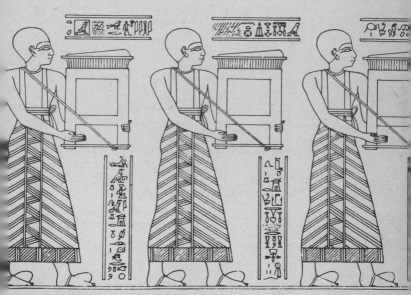

THE SACRED ACTIVITIES

Whoever has visited Egypt remembers the astonishing spectacle of the *mastabas* of Saqqara: outside, the scorching sun harshly lights a world of desolation: crumbling monuments and mountains of sand with an unbearable brightness; in the tombs, on the other hand, there is a delicious freshness, and the sudden resurrection of a world as old as the pyramids; on a compressed and miniature scale, a multitude of men move, work, sing, under the amused but vigilant eye of the master. . . . We are in the rich estate of a great person of ancient times, and a crowd of servants and domestics surround him and busy themselves in his honor. He is just getting up; a domestic adjusts his wig, another massages his feet, a third presents his clothes to him; several dwarf servants choose the collar that he will wear, while harpists and singers entertain him with their melody. . . . But already the work is beginning, and the stewards present their report to him: a hard day is ahead, passed in inspecting the vast estate where the lord lives and which he must make prosper.

This life of the great feudal lord, all-powerful in his own domain, living in his castle, in the midst of a crowd of attentive servants, was the life attributed by the Egyptians to their gods: the supreme being, come to earth, lived in a vast palace, the 'castle of the god'; the 'servants of the god' – the priests – ac-

77

The high priest Nebounnef

corded him the care that any high personage required; from rising to retiring, he was washed, dressed, perfumed, fed, distracted by songs and music, put in good humor, so that he could accomplish his office of god: to assure the proper working of the universe. It is this domestic service to a superior being that the priests must perform.

But the lord is all-powerful here, and does not let himself be approached as a simple country squire; his good or bad humor does not merely decide the fate of a few dozen peasants: his anger can cause the end of humanity. . . . A divine power does not know how to live with impunity on the earth, where so many impurities, so many evil forces can strike or injure him. . . . Every precaution has to be taken to assure, in the most secret of the sanctuaries, far from the eyes and the impurities of the world, the integrity of the divine presence. Solitude, purity of the temple and of the ministers, absolute rigor in the exercise of the religion, punctual regularity of offerings, such are the conditions indispensable to the satisfaction of the divinity – such are the unvarying principles which govern all the cults of Egypt.

Egypt sleeps. Over the towns, the fields, over the Nile and the desert, silence reigns. Meanwhile, behind the high walls of the sacred enclosure, on the terrace of the temple, a man takes his vigil: he is the watcher of the constellations, who notes, at the setting of the stars, the shedding of the nocturnal hours. The night passes; it is time. . . .

At his signal, a whole quarter of the divine domain awakes; lights appear, fires are lit, life resumes. In a few hours, the sacred service will commence, all must be ready. And the workshops, the stores, the bakeries are stirring: the scribes bring to the overseer the list of offerings of the day which are coming; haste is necessary. And while the ovens are lit, the cakes and breads are prepared, the butchers kill the beast of sacrifice, which a veterinary-priest has pronounced pure; fruits and vegetables are prepared, heaped on plates; accountants busy themselves recording all the produce promised for the offering, chaplains purify the pieces of meat with water from the sacred wells; in the buzzing animation of the workshops, the hours pass, marked by the clear call of the *sereno* perched on his terrace, and already the sky whitens in the east.

Then another quarter of the religious community stirs: here

are the priests who leave their dwellings and, in little groups visible in the still dense shadows by the whiteness of their linen robes, go toward the sacred lake; by the four lateral ramps they go down to the water where a light fog floats. In making their ablutions, not only do they purify their bodies but divine life little by little enters them: the sacred water, like the primordial sea from which the world came in the beginning, is regenerative: whoever is sprinkled with it feels himself invaded by a new power, raised from this life below to the eternal world where the gods reside. . . .

They are going to enter this world; a first door, in the sandstone wall which surrounds the temple, and they are in the

Sacred lake of Karnak

great outer walk which encircles the sacred edifice; there, they separate, each going to his post. Renewing the water in the reserve basin, lighting incense, and doing various purifications – every preliminary service is done in the lateral sacristies and on the path which the offering procession will soon follow. Meanwhile time goes on: the sky, now completely light, reddens on the east bank.

Then the offering procession arrives. The workshops have made haste; punctual as always, at the prescribed moment they deliver the morning food which will be offered to the gods, and the carriers advance toward the side corridor of the temple, holding before them, on their bent arms, platters heavy with flowers and fruit, or, balanced on their head, the heavy loads of breads and meats which the divine appetite requires, and the pitchers of beer or wine which will quench the divine thirst. Led by a chanting officiant, the procession advances into the temple, whose doors open one by one; the prayer rises, consecrating the food to the gods of the temple and inviting them to receive it. Having arrived in the altar room in the center of the temple, not far from the sanctuary, the bearers stop; they put their platters on the tables and the altars, placing the jugs on stands, heaping up this display with offerings of flowers and green plants.

And while the bearers withdraw, and the priests purify and consecrate the offerings with holy water and incense, another phase of the cult commences.

From the narrow windows near the ceiling several rays of light enter the altar room; before the priests and the chanters remaining by the offerings stands the massive facade of a sanctuary still closed. An officiant of high rank, who alone can enter into the presence of the god, then mounts the several steps which separate him from the sanctuary and breaks the clay which, since the day before, prevented entrance; he pushes the bolt, opens the doors, and as the sun appears above the horizon and begins its ascent in the eastern sky, the leading chanter intones before the god the morning hymn: *Rise thou, great god, in peace! Rise, thou art in peace.*

And the answering chanters, in an immense chorus which vibrates the aged beams of the ceilings and reverberates from chapel to chapel in a vast roaring echo:

Thou art risen, thou art in peace; rise thou beautifully in peace,

wake thou, god of this city, to life! The gods have arisen to honor thy soul, O holy winged disc who rises from his mother Nout! It is thou who breaks thy prison of clay to spread on the earth thy powdered gold, thou who rise in the east, then sink in the west and sleep in thy temple each day. . . .

Then the soloist resumes his short invocation, as the chorus, unvaryingly, after each verse, repeats its refrain. The divine epithets exhausted, the head of the chanters goes on to the associated gods, then to the parts of the divine body which waken into life: 'Thine eyes cast flame! Thine eyes illuminate the night! Thy brows wake in beauty, O radiant visage which knows not anger!'

Forty-five times the divine organs which renew the day were thus invoked, and as many times the chorus took up their refrain: 'Thou art risen, thou art in peace . . . thou spreadest o'er the earth thy powdered gold.'

FACE TO FACE

Meanwhile the priest who, alone, has the right to approach the god, has entered the sanctuary; the darkness is deep; the candle, lit the evening before, is consumed little by little, then the night returns. To one side, the sacred ship on its pedestal; in the center, the naos, a small edifice of granite or of basalt, closed by a double door of wood. Elsewhere, a chest of wood where the utensils necessary to the cult are kept and the altar on which the platter of offerings from the previous evening rests.

The priest changes the candle and lights it; the fantastic shadows are cast by the ship, the naos, the officiant; they move about on the engraved walls which are painted in vivid colors: life returns to the sanctuary, after the long nocturnal lethargy. Then he breaks the clay seal on the doors of the naos, carefully draws toward him the two doors, and – a solemn moment – the image of the god leaves the night at the precise instant the sun emerges on the horizon, with the first words of the morning hymn. . . .

All those who have walked through the rooms of the Louvre museum certainly recall the little chapel which has been placed there with its statue of the god Osiris; the god appears in his niche, skillfully lit by side lamps. The visitor is impressed by the strange aspect of this wooden figure leaping from the shadow, crude and awkward but singularly fascinating. This is

83

Statuette of the cult of Osiris
(Louvre Museum)

the way the god must have appeared when the priest set aside the doors of the naos, a shape indistinct in the shadow, but shining with the brilliance of its jeweled eyes, its crown, its metallic decoration, and jewelry.

To contemplate the god was not an ordinary privilege. In principle only the sovereign, son of the divinity, was able to do so; in fact, in each temple, a small number of priests – the highest in rank – could substitute for the king and see, face to face, each morning, the venerable idol where the divine power came to reside. In placing his hands on the statue, in a sort of embrace, the priest 'rendered his soul' to him; the god, visible in the Egyptian sky, resuming possession of his earthly resting place to reign all day in his temple, representing in the naos what he was in the universe.

Then the priest prayed, arms falling the length of the body, in an attitude of respectful humility; repeating four times his formula so that it could reach the four points of the horizon, the extreme limits of the world: 'I worship thy Majesty, with the chosen words, with the prayers which increase thy prestige, in thy great names and in the holy manifestations under which thou revealed thyself the first day of the world.'

THE MEAL OF THE GOD

The offerings, meanwhile, always waited on the altars so the god could fully satisfy himself. The priest then withdrew, within the sanctuary, the platter of the evening before, and went to refill it in the altar room with fresh breads and cakes: only this symbolic collection entered near the god, representing the entire collection of meats, cakes, vegetables, and fruits heaped up on the tables. Then, in two symbolic acts, the offering of incense and the offering of Maat, the return to the god of his bounty and of the universe where his power reigned was accomplished.

Obviously the food was not consumed by the divinity: only a part of his immaterial soul is present in his statue: the meal of the god took place therefore outside the limits of human perception: the spirit of the food passes into the divine spirit, without any apparent change in the offerings heaped on the altars. . . . When the god, at the end of a fixed time, would be satisfied – and with him the secondary divinities which surround him in his temple – the offerings would be placed on the altars of all the statues of high personages who had obtained the privilege of seeing their effigy in the sacred place, then they would return to the workshops to be divided up according to a set system, among the various priests of the temple. The divine personnel thus lived on the offerings consecrated to the god, contenting themselves with their material reality, after the divinity and the privileged dead would satisfy themselves with the symbolic 'essence.' In establishing the earthly foundations for a divinity, the Pharaohs thus at the same time assured the feeding of the god and the subsistence of the sacred personnel who served him. But the clergy, sometimes less scrupulous, had a tendency to utilize these revenues directly, without previously submitting them to divine enjoyment. Thus the texts spell out carefully that *one lives on the provisions of the gods; but this is always food which leaves the altar after the god is satisfied* [Temple of Edfu.]

THE PERSONAL CARE OF THE GOD

The meal finished, the toilet begins: the god is washed, his clothes of the previous evening are removed, he is dressed in new material, then he is painted.

We know that all material was not acceptable to the gods and the priests: wool, in particular, could not under any circumstances be brought near the consecrated beings and objects. It is the byssus, the fine linen, which alone served to clothe the sacred personnel; it is this also which furnished the necessary material for the divine statues. To this end, weaving workshops were annexed to the sanctuaries, whose sole function was to prepare the cult materials; the historical documents cite this on occasion: those of the town of Sais, in the Delta, are particularly celebrated; in the Greco-Roman epoch, the papyri testify abundantly to the quarrels between temples and the sovereign over the quotas of production for the sacred workshops.

These shops furnished the temple regularly, where a room, the 'chamber of materials,' was consecrated to storing reserve clothing. Finally a specialized priest, the stolist, 'the one who enters the sanctuary to dress the gods with their apparel,' had charge of these materials and the monopoly on their use.

The toilet of the god is continued then by the successive offering of four strips of material of fine linen, first placed in the wood casket in the sanctuary; the white fabric first, then the blue, the green, and finally the red. In practice, the divine clothing was not renewed each day; it was only done at the

Weaving house (Old Egyptian model)

solemn services which took place once or twice a week. But daily the symbolic offering of the four strips of material took place.

It was the same with the finery which was only offered to the god at feast services; let us recall here what this finery consists of.

Each temple contained a small room, carefully shut off

at ordinary times, which bore the name of *treasury*. There the most precious objects of the cult were kept, and the material attributes of the divinity: pectoral plaques, necklaces of all kinds, miniature headdresses, reproducing all the innumerable elements which could ornament the chief of a god, symbolic offerings of the *oudja* eye, of the clepsydre, timbrels and *menat* necklaces, scepters and bracelets. These diverse objects were made of the finest material, gold or silver, encrusted with lapis lazuli, or of enameled paste of every color, sometimes worked with the greatest artistry by talented jewelers. These objects were brought out only on the most solemn occasions, and the stolist presented them then one by one to the god, after having clothed him with fine linen, to complete the display. But at the daily morning service, these precious offerings were not presented.

A final ceremony ended the divine toilet; the anointment of the god with the cosmetic oil *medjet*. Holding in his left hand the little flacon of alabaster which contained the precious ointment, the priest plunged in the little finger of his right hand, then touched the brow of the divine statue with this finger, pronouncing the sacred formula.

At this point in the ritual, the divine toilet is practically over; the god, washed, clothed, ornamented and smeared with the perfumed oil – satiated by excess – could brave anew the dark of the sanctuary: the divine forces were sustained, preserved from all injury, able to carry on, for another day, their cosmic role.

THE FINAL CEREMONIES OF THE MORNING RITUAL

A certain number of ritual gestures remain to be done, but are rapidly executed: the main work is done. Several sprinklings of water, on the naos, the statue, the sanctuary, assure a surfeit of material purity; then the priest presents the five grains of natron (natron of the 'Valley of Salt,' the present Wady Natroun, and natron from distant El Kab in Upper Egypt), then five grains of another nitrous salt, and five grains of resin. He veils again the face of the god in his naos, shuts its doors, which he bolts and seals off with clay until the next day. Finally, before withdrawing, after a last fumigation with incense which purifies the air of all hostile presences, he empties what remains in his container on the ground and sweeps away the traces of steps imprinted on the sand covering the ground. This done, he withdraws, leaving the naos closed, the platter of breads on the altar, the candle which little by little disappears, and shuts the door of the sanctuary on its precious contents. The morning service is ended.

The scrupulous following of these ceremonies, the recitations and hymns, putting the temple in order after the morning service, all required time. The sun was already high in the sky when, leaving the remote chambers of the sanctuary, the priests rediscovered the brilliance of the Egyptian sky. They were more or less free until the noonday service. What did they do until then? It is probable that they refreshed themselves with food: the offerings had made the tour of the altars of the god and of the tables of the high personages represented by their statues; returned to the workshops, they were waiting to be consumed. Then, they could busy themselves with the many side duties that their function as priests entailed, internal administration, inventories, reports, problems relating to construction or repairs of the sacred buildings, and finally, ecclesiastical justice. The midday service came to rescue them from these innumerable duties.

THE MIDDAY SERVICE

The midday service was shorter than the great morning one. All the care the god required had already been, in effect, bestowed; thus the sanctuary remained shut; the gods received no more meals before sundown. The noon service had as its purpose to emphasize by religious ceremony the cosmic instant, vital in the life of the god, when the sun at the height of its course began to decline, rather than to add any further ceremony to those which had already gratified the sacred effigies at dawn.

The midday service consisted essentially of sprinkling water and incense before the tabernacles of the secondary gods, of the deified sovereigns worshiped in the temple next to the gods, and – all around the sanctuary – before the little rooms consecrated to associated cults. Purification of the containers, renewal of the water in the basin which was always full – a sort of holy-water fount – in the altar room, libations, incensing of various points defined by the ritual, were all part of the midday service.

THE EVENING SERVICE

As to the evening service, if it took on more ceremony, it still remained very much less solemn than the morning service. It was, roughly, a repetition of the first service of the day, except that the sanctuary remained shut and all the ceremonies took place in the side chapels around the holy of holies: carrying of offerings, consecration, libations, incense, withdrawal of food, final purifications: nearly all the elements of the morning ritual were repeated; then, on a final fumigation, the doors of the chapel and corridors were shut; the priests withdrew and while the darkness rapidly descended over the valley, the gods of the temple, like the human beings, gave themselves up to sleep. Alone on the terrace, the astronomer priest measured by the successive sweep of the constellations the hours of the nocturnal sky.

The daily cult as we have described it was rendered, simultaneously and in almost the same form, in all the temples of Egypt. It goes without saying that the fullness of the ceremonies, the number of participants, the richness of the alimentary offerings, were evidence of the importance of a sanctuary; it was in the modest chapels with one or two ministers that ostentation had little scope; everything leads us to believe that the *spirit* of the three daily services as they have been described was nevertheless respected here. At least we can state that in the great temples, Karnak, Abydos, Edfu (to which we are essentially referring), Dendereh, Philae, the liturgy was performed in a parallel fashion, at the same moments of the day, with nearly identical rites, only the epithets and divine names being modified. According to the case, certain details of the cult took a more or less important place: thus, we have included in this rather theoretical picture a few recitations or liturgical rituals which only appeared at solemn services every four of five days; we have, in exchange, neglected a few secondary details too peculiar to a given temple to include in a reconstruction of the cults of all Egypt. But the general picture which remains certainly does not go very much astray from what actually occurred every day in the great majority of sanctuaries.

As it appears to us, the divine Egyptian cult was not devoid of grandeur. Certainly a good part of its phases can seem purely material, and the picture of gods who are washed, dressed, and fed does not correspond to a very spiritual conception of the cult. On the other hand, the essential of the symbolism related to the ablutions, to the worth of the fumigations, to the import of the invocations, escapes us; to make sense of them, one needs explanations we cannot go into here. But to limit the Egyptian cult to these two impressions would certainly be unjust.

We have noted, in the appropriate places, the parallelism between the movements of the heavens, of the sun, and of the stars, and the various liturgical acts; one must understand that the priests were not constrained to entertain, in their temples, an idol afflicted with human needs and appetites, but rather thought to preserve, infused in a statue, a part of the divine all-powerful, visible even in life and the movements of the universe. Every important moment in the course of the sun called forth a special ceremony dedicated to the earthly embodiment of this divine radiance: the transposition, even in the location of a temple and in the ordering of rites, of the essential phases of a universal movement, surely does not lack poetry or grandeur.

This said, it remains undeniable that in the aspect that the texts have revealed to us, the cult is principally a succession of formal acts, determined in a given order by the ritual and performed at a fixed hour: everything is foreseen, everything defined: the moment, the place, the dress, the gesture, the formula. Like the service of the great lord we pictured at the beginning of this chapter, it corresponds much more to a series of rituals than to an internal spiritual exercise. The cult is an element – indispensable – to the religious life, but only *one* of these elements. The people, it is interesting to note, do not participate in any of the daily acts of the divine service; this is an affair of technicians – a very special act in the religious life, which only depicts one of its aspects, the least personal. The rich individual spirituality that one sometimes finds in the ministers of the temples is expressed in other circumstances. As to collective fervor, which is excluded from the holy place and whose extent so far we have not evaluated, this is shown in religious ceremonies outside the temple.

The daily cult of the gods within the temples did not constitute the sole religious activity of the priests. Frequently, every four or five days, a solemn service replaced the regular one: this already necessitated much more pomp and an appreciable extension of rites, but more than this it easily doubled the appearances of the god, that is to say in processions outside the temple, during which the statue of the god, enclosed in a little chapel of wood placed on a ship, was carried on the shoulders of the priests throughout the village.

The ship was a model reduced from the much more important one in which the god could sail on the Nile and make occasional long voyages. In ordinary times, it was placed in the sanctuary of the god on a little pedestal of stone; in certain temples with larger proportions, a room open at both ends served as a 'garage' for the ship, or even, as is the case at Karnak, a special structure might be built for it.

It was decorated at the stem and at the stern with a head of the divinity it carried: Hathor of the smiling features, the falcon Horus, Khons at the helm surmounted by the lunar disc, each according to the particular cult. At the center was fixed the light wood tabernacle where cloth was stretched on little columns. At the stern, as in a normal boat, the oarsman held a long side oar which served as a rudder: sometimes it was an image of the god; before the naos, a kneeling figure gave permanent homage to the enclosed god; finally, toward the front, there were several sacred emblems on shields, varying according to the temple: an upright sphinx, a falcon, and others.

This ship could have varying dimensions. In general it was smaller than those of the boats on the Nile. Let us not forget that it had to be carried on men's backs, often a rather long

Sacred ship (Karnak)

distance, and it also had to be kept in the interior of the sanctuaries. Usually it was rather small. But certain scenes of the great temples show us an imposing ship which required no less than thirty carriers . . . .

As the title of 'carrier of the ship' appears in a number of inferior religious offices, it is probable that at the processions of these giant ships the men took turns under the shafts: thus they won some glory in the eyes of their fellow citizens, and virtue in the heart of the divinity: 'I carried Ptah at arm's length,' an Egyptian of the Ramesside epoch tells us. 'Power given me by the god to be beatified with his favor!' But if one lacked spiritual benefits, one could always strike up a friendship, as was the case with a certain Moses, whose stela preserved at Toulouse tells us that he made the acquaintance of a companion in carrying the ship of a god with him. . . . Before the ship walked the chaplain, incense burner in hand, spreading the fumes from the turpentine grains to chase away the evil spirits which could prowl alongside the ship. Behind followed the priests, impressive in their immaculate linen clothing, perhaps chanting some sacred hymn. And around them moved the crowd of the faithful and the idle, noisy and excited, giving out shouts of joy or joining their voices with those of the sacred singers. The town of Luxor has preserved something of this ancient rite when at the local feast of Abou'l Haggag, the patron saint of the city, they continue to draw a boat along the side streets – although a carriage equipped with wheels transports it.

THE STATIONS

At these solemn outings, the god did not make his trip in one stretch, to return directly to his sanctuary: every hundred meters, his itinerary was marked out with 'stations' where little street altars received his ship. The carriers rested here a while, while the priests, facing the tabernacle, performed the prescribed rites (in general fumigations, diverse offerings, readings from the holy books). It is on this occasion also that the oracles were given out by written consultations. In the evening, the god returned to the temple, or he received hospitality in some chapel, to resume his wanderings the following day.

Such manifestations were far from being rare: the religious calendars that many temples preserved show us that, according to the season, each month contained from five to ten outings of this kind, now to one and now to another of the gods of the vicinity; the journey varied according to the end of the procession and the temple chosen for the night's stop.

In other circumstances, the outing of the god was made without a ship: at Bouta (in the Delta), we know for example that the god Min, dressed in red and protected by a breastplate, presented himself at the street altars in a chariot drawn by horses – while the crowd, conscious of assisting in an important episode of the divine movement, trembled with holy terror. . . .

Finally, the god was drawn in a chariot by the faithful themselves, and an entire act from mythological history was played out on this occasion. This was the case at the feasts of Papremis, where Herodotus tells us the priests exchanged such violent blows in honor of their divinity that certain of them died from their wounds.

One sees the priestly life sometimes carried with it a few risks. At least in usual practice the functions of the priests, at the popular feasts, were more pacific. Their role varied according to the nature of the festivities. Guardians of the god at these outings, they had also a few rites to execute during the halts in the processions, several religious acts to perform in connection with the object itself of the feast, for these feasts could be dedicated to all sorts of events: the coming of the floods (feast of the Nile) and harvest feasts – in harmony with the events of the agricultural year, feasts of drunkenness, feasts of Osiris, feasts of Amon of Luxor – in memory of the episodes in the life of the gods; feasts of the Valley at Thebes – dedicated to the cult of the dead gods and to the deceased of the city of the dead; finally special feasts at each sanctuary commemorating the triumph of the god over his enemies, insuring the annual installation of a new sacred animal, accompanying on the first day of the year the union of the god and his earthly effigy. . . . Certain of these feasts were public and displayed from chapel to chapel, in the midst of popular merriment. Others were secret, and hid their episodes in the interior of the enclosures. In all, however, the priests remained essentially *the servants* of the divinity, assuring his service in the temple and outside the temple: at these outings, the participation of the crowd was purely formal: they acclaimed the god and rejoiced in his passing, but did not contribute, to speak of, in the ceremonies required. It is only on very particular occasions – at the oracular consultations – that we see the priests serve as intermediaries between the god and the human beings who worshipped him.

In certain circumstances the popular religion, the personal faith of the laymen, needed the offices of the clergy. The divine cult and the belief of the masses then found a common ground: when one wished to consult the god and solicit his advice. In a dispute between two adversaries, or in defining a line of conduct for the future, the divine clairvoyance is a sovereign resort, omniscient, omnipresent. The god knows, in fact, better than human beings, how to discern the true from the false and how to predict future events: in his perfect integrity, he is not sensitive to the social conditions of the plaintiffs, does not distinguish between poor and rich in making his judgments. 'O Amon-Re,' says a hymn of the New Kingdom, 'thou art the judge of the unfortunate, who takes not the gifts of the violent. . . .'

Also the custom of recourse to the oracles took on, in the New Kingdom, considerable importance. Carriers of the divine word, interpreters of his will, the priests from that time on had to play a prominent role in society.

The fact is that it was not always easy to question the god; but a number of techniques were used.

THE ORACLE OF THE SHIP

One of the techniques most generally used consisted of soliciting the advice of the divinity at the time of his outings. We have pictured already the feast days and those on which the god left his sanctuary to pay a visit to his colleague gods. From street altar to street altar, in the midst of a great crowd, the ship carrying the divine statue borne aloft on the shoulders of the bearers was acclaimed by the faithful. It was the most propitious occasion to question the god. Breaking through the mob, the plaintiffs attempted to approach the ship; and when silence was gradually established around them and sufficient awe had filled them, they addressed themselves directly to the divinity: 'My good lord, is it correct that I stole such and such an object from so-and-so?' A moment of anguish followed, more or less prolonged, according to the time that the god took to examine the question within himself. And suddenly the bearers felt the divine will enter them. According to the case, those at the stem felt their burden weighing them down, becoming unsupportable, and had to bow under the leaden weight. If the god leaned also, he approved; in other circumstances, the bearers saw themselves pushed to the fore or brusquely forced to withdraw, always at the instigation of the god present in the ship: if he wished to go forward, the response was positive; backward, it was negative. When one of the petitioners had been approved by the oracle, his rival could 'counterquestion' to try to regain the advantage; but even if the god consecrated his defeat by a new affirmation, the plaintiff did not consider himself completely beaten. He could renew his questions with another god on a similar outing, or before another street altar; the priests of the different clergies did not always represent the same tendency, and the petitioner could hope to see some god show himself more conciliatory. . . .

This curious practice seems to have corresponded to a very profound tendency in the Egyptian people. In fact we were a

95

little surprised to read, some years ago, in a journal from Cairo, the echo of an incident which threw a village in Upper Egypt into an uproar, and which arose undoubtedly from the same sociological source as the ancient rites which we are going to describe. Under the attractive title of 'Coffin Which Dances (sic) On Air,' the author of the article recounts the following facts: a village was in mourning for a venerable old man weighted with years and wisdom who had passed on to a better world; after the customary tears and cries, duly rolled in his matting and packed in his coffin, the old sheik was in his final dwelling. Under his bed of state, the voluntary carriers took turns from minute to minute, each wanting to carry the holy man to the cemetery. All went admirably and the procession advanced to the middle of the funerary litanies, when the coffin began to tremble and the bearers collapsed under a sheik as heavy, all of a sudden, as a load of rocks. . . . The event merited reflection. It was discussed noisily, with the expressive vigor necessary in Upper Egypt, and the conclusion was that the honorable deceased preferred to take another route to his final resting place. The convoy then made a half-turn, took a parallel side road, with the dead miraculously lightened. Then suddenly the coffin gave way again nearly to the point of its first tumble. With the anguish increasing, and the evident presence of the supernatural filling the crowd with a holy terror, it was necessary to stop and consider. They affirmed then that the old sheik had twice refused to pass before – or behind – the house of his own family. . . . This information evaluated and a thorough investigation made, it was revealed that the death of the old man was not as natural as it had first appeared, and that his good relative had precipitated the issue somewhat. And justice was done, with the promptness without recourse that the fellahs of the Said apply to the regulation of their family affairs. In stirring twice, the deceased had, from the beyond, indicated his assassin to his fellow citizens. . . . Customs, one sees, are tenacious; three thousand years earlier, in similar fashion, the god in his ship indicated his wishes by dictating the necessary movements to his carriers.

THE PROPHETIC VOICES

However, the ship did not go out every day, and there were some complex questions that a simple negative or affirmative reply could not resolve. In these cases, one addressed the god directly, who replied in his own voice. For the Egyptians of these times, the gods were not as inaccessible as one might believe; no doubt they were not encountered as often as in Greece, where every old man seated along a road, or every slightly alluring woman, might feign to be Zeus in a merry mood or Aphrodite in quest of strong emotions. But sometimes one encountered, at the edge of a lake, some strange apparition rendering one foolish with terror, like the shepherd who saw a goddess, in the simplest attire, come out of the roses under his very eyes. Ordinarily, however, the gods wisely dwelt in their temples, and it was there that they were consulted.

The little private chapel which was established, in the late epochs, on the terrace above the temple of Deir el Bahari, facing Luxor, was set up, for example, for such consultations. The chapel consists of two successive rooms, separated by a door. The pilgrims – in emergency, the sick who came to seek a cure from the god Amenophis – remained in the exterior room; the god lived in the second. During the night, when the little group of crippled waited patiently for the god to cure them, a solemn and somewhat terrifying voice came from the sanctuary and carried to each one the remedy for his ill. For the vault which surmounts the door is pierced by a sort of window through which some priest, concealed in the sanctuary, interpreted the divine will. . . . The sick, as a general rule, did not doubt the supernatural intervention; but there were sometimes strong characters who would only believe what they could verify: a Greek writer, particularly picturesque, tells us how a pilgrim named Athenodorus, praying in the common room of the chapel, heard a voice coming from the sanctuary; the brave man, soldier of his state, had had to learn a vigorous objectivity in the guard corps. Instead of being satisfied, he had the indecency to go and open the door, to see who was speaking. . . . The priests had evidently foreseen such contingencies, and had provided themselves with wise retreats; thus it was that our centurion saw nothing untoward, and ended up being strongly impressed. Having, by this excess, regained health, he decided that the incident was well worth noting.

Among strangers, in fact, belief in prophetic dreams was often enough wavering; if certain Greeks accepted voluntarily the principles of the Egyptian religion to the point sometimes of participating in its beliefs, a good number of others only carried their faith as far as they could verify it. One finds sometimes, in the papyri, the expression of their disillusion and scepticism. 'I swear by Sarapis, if it were not that I still have some respect for you, you would never see me again. Everything you say is false, as is everything your gods say, for they have put us in a fine pickle, and each time your visions announce that we are going to be saved, we are sunk a little further into it.' [Papyrus of Serapeum, no. 70.] Before such a spiritual state, no doubt widespread, we can believe that the priests of Deir el Bahari persuaded the credulous Athenodorus to inscribe the story of his misadventure on the temple walls. . . .

Other temples, for example that of Karanis at Fayoum, presented acts comparable to this of Deir el Bahari; certain divine statues, on the other hand, were hollow and had an acoustical passage through which a man, concealed behind the god, could speak in his name.

The technique may have been very generally widespread; the texts are numerous in which we see a man going to pass a night in the sacred edifice to receive from the god some prophetic dream which will reveal to him what he ought to do. This was the case with the sick; but it was also that of women desiring a child. The demotic story of Satni reports, for example, that the lady Mehitouskhet was greatly grieved not to have any descendants; in despair, she went to spend a night in the temple of Imouthes, the great healer, and she had a dream:

> One spoke to her, saying: Are you not Mehitousket, the wife of Satni, who sleeps in the temple to receive a remedy for your sterility through the grace of god? Tomorrow go to the fountain of Satni, your husband, and you will find a foot of colocase sprouting there. The colocase that you find, you will pull up with its leaves, you will make a remedy from it which will give you to your husband, then you will lie next to him and you will conceive of him this same night.

At her awakening, the lady followed to the letter the advice of the god, and her wishes were promptly fulfilled.

The priests, one sees, did not lack work, even during the night. . . . This old belief that the night in the temple, with or without divine revelation, was propitious for conception is very far from extinct: in the course of four winters that we spent in the temple of Esna, in Upper Egypt, copying out the inscriptions, it often happened that women of the village entered the great hypostyle room and with conviction went around the columns seven times under the sleepy eye of the ghafir, convinced that this operation would assure them early issue. . . . Do not the hieroglyphic texts of the great temple state that the god *gives sons to whoever calls upon him and daughters to whoever entreats him?*

But the priests, bearers of the word of the god, sometimes had to deal with more complex questions. The same story of Satni shows us, for example, a magician at the end of his cunning before a more skillful colleague. He puts to sea, and lands at Hermopolis, the city of the god Thoth; he goes to pray to the god in his temple to come to his aid, and the god, in a dream, reveals to him the place where he can find and copy out the all-powerful formulas which he himself uses. On awakening, the magician moved according to the instructions of the god, and everything went off as it had been told to him.

The god sometimes found a more direct way of expressing himself: he entered the body of a man or an infant, making him go into a trance and through this intermediary dictating his will. The story of Ounamon describes such a case of sacred madness; later, we know that infants and fakirs finding refuge in the temples served as mediums for transmitting the word of the god.

OTHER ORACULAR TECHNIQUES

There was no end to priestly resources for interpreting the will of the god to the people. Still other techniques were employed, in particular those which consisted of presenting written requests to the god. An oracular text dating from the high priest Pinedjem reveals to us the consultation in these terms. A priest of Amon was suspected of having some little diggings for his personal use in the granaries of the god; in the course of a procession of the ship, two written statements were drawn up in the presence of Amon. One reads: 'O Amon-Re, king of the gods, my good lord! they say that Tuthmosis, this superintendent of properties, is in possession of something that can no longer be recovered.' The other is drawn up thus: 'O Amon-Re, king of the gods, my good lord! they say that Tuthmosis, this superintendent of properties, is in possession of nothing that can not be recovered.' The high priest then prayed that the god judge. The great god fully consented, and the two statements were placed before him. He chose the second statement. This was verified a second time, and the god repeated his choice.

The accused thus recovered his honor with this proof, and benefited a little later by an important advancement. . . .

This technique is evident in connection with a number of inscribed fragments found at the time of the French excavations of Deir el Medineh. On little pieces of pottery or limestone, the petitioner wrote his question: it could relate to the most diverse subjects. Some of these were as follows:

> Is this veal good enough for me to accept?
> Will the minister of state give us a new leader now?
> Will they let me become the leader?
> Have I told a lie?
> Will I receive disapproval?
> Have the soldiers stolen?
> My good lord, is one of my goats at the house of Ptahmose?

Advancement, commerce, professional activity, town robbery, every subject was brought before the god, and he had to reply to every question. How did he do it? A fragment that we found in 1951 seems to give the solution: he gave out only one word: '*No.*' No doubt the god would choose between two responses, *yes* and *no*, and his priest transmitted the divine verdict to the questioner.

This custom, current in the New Kingdom, was still in favor a thousand years later; in fact, in the little temple of the god Soknopaios, at Fayoum, questions addressed to the god by the inhabitants of the area were found: the problems were very much the same as those of their distant ancestors: sales and purchases, questions of taxes, and even matrimonial advice: 'Will it be granted to me to marry Madame X and will she not be the wife of another? Reveal this to me and heed this little written prayer. . . .'

THE ORACLE OF THE SACRED ANIMALS

Oracles from the statue, from the divine ships, prophetic voices, dreams, the processes used to question the god were extremely varied. Even his sacred animal could be called on to transmit the reply of the god. This was the case of the bull Apis. In general he was let out of his stable only once a day, to allow him a little diversion – which also permitted him, among other benefits, to be exhibited to tourists in exchange for a fair remuneration. Strabo reports:

100

At a certain hour every day, Apis is let out into his court, chiefly to be shown to strangers, for as well as one can see him through a window in his quarters, strangers very much prefer to see him outside at liberty; but after he has been left to run and jump a while in his yard, he is brought back into his house. . . .

No doubt the movements of the bull were interpreted in a prophetic sense; the texts are numerous which tell us that Apis revealed the future to whoever consulted him. At Medamoud, in a temple of the Greco-Roman epoch uncovered by French excavations, a little 'oratory' was discovered in which the sacred bull of the vicinity replied to questions submitted to him.

The oracle of the Bull at Medamoud

JUSTICE GIVEN OUT AT THE GATE OF THE TEMPLES

If the questions to which the priests had to reply in the name of their god could be of every sort, we have nevertheless seen that the divine oracle often had to settle judicial questions; frequently, in the New Kingdom, trials were held in the temples or in their immediate vicinity. In addition the priests sat, next to the local functionaries, on the tribunals of each town (decree of Horemheb). In the late epoch, it was the general custom to appeal, perhaps for certain affairs which were more religious than civil, to the justice of the god; the propylaea of the temples received at this time the name of 'gate where justice is rendered,' and the texts specify that 'this is the place where requests of all plaintiffs are heard, the weak and the powerful are judged, to distinguish between justice and iniquity.' One of the kiosks resting against the façade of the great temple of Medamoud seems to be one of these ecclesiastical tribunals. What causes were especially reserved to the evaluation of the god? On which were the priests qualified to pronounce sentence? And how did the administration regard these tribunal officials? We cannot say, for lack of documentation; but the survival up to recent years of the religious tribunals in Islamic Egypt, in the presence of state justice, shows that the coexistence of two jurisdictions in specialized functions is perfectly conceivable.

Like their ancestors who carried the ships, whose shoulders were sensitive to the slightest movements of the god, the priests of the last centuries of paganism took their role of interpreters of the divine will very seriously.

Finally, there were *official missions* which sent the priests out from the temples to travel across the country. Sometimes these missions were religious, sometimes political.

The former took place at the great feasts of the neighboring temples. As independent as these sanctuaries could appear, to our eyes, each dedicated to a group of particular divinities, there was sometimes a relationship among them which facilitated the administration of properties, or associated the cults under a common leadership – or even created from distant associations a kinship of certain cults. The temples of the two towns of Khemmis (Askhmim) and Abydos, for example, could be occasionally ruled by the same priest; the proximity of the cities permitted this without great harm; the case was still more usual for the two neighboring towns of Memphis and Letopolis, which in the low epochs frequently had a superior clergy in common. The priests appointed to these twin offices obviously had to spend a notable part of their life in travel.

In other circumstances, the relationship of two cults, even geographically removed from each other, led to frequent contacts between the clergies of both; this was the case, for example, of the cities of Edfu and Dendereh, where the falcon god Horus and his wife the lovely goddess Hathor were worshiped. Each year, at the feast of the 'happy reunion,' the goddess left her temple at Dendereh and, after sailing ninety miles, rejoined her divine husband for two weeks in his city of Edfu. During the voyage, from town to town, the parade gathered new boats, each important temple finding it opportune to send one of its representatives to assist in the sacred marriage. The several boats from Dendereh were followed and surrounded at the end of the trip by an incalculable number of official ships carrying the delegations of friendly clergies, and no doubt by a crowd of private feluccas whose occupants wanted to assist in the annual rite and to profit from the general merriment and the commercial business which would accompany it. . . .

Other meetings of the priests had a more clearly administrative and political aspect. Despite their diversity and their apparent autonomy, all the Egyptian cults were grouped, administratively, under the direction of a superior of the prophets of the double country: one could believe then in the existence of an *Egyptian clergy* whose superior interests surpassed the minor individual problems of the provincial chapels. The sovereign made sure of holding this clergy's loyalty. In various circumstances, for example, a circular called together a priest from each temple to constitute a kind of sacred assembly accompanying the king in ceremonies or trips. This was the case in the year 4 of Psamtik II, when on the day following his Nubian expedition the sovereign wished to put in an appearance in an Asiatic country:

> Messages were sent to the great temples of Upper and Lower Egypt saying: 'Pharaoh is leaving for the country of Khor in Syria. Have the priests come with presents from the gods of Egypt to carry to the country of Khor with the Pharaoh.' A message was subsequently sent also to Teudjoi saying: 'Have a priest come with the present of Amon to go to the country of Khor with the Pharaoh.' The priests assembled and agreed to say to Peteisis: 'It is you who have been chosen to go with the Pharaoh; there is no one else in the city who can do it. You are scribe in the House of Life, and it is a thing one can ask of you to which you can only give an agreeable answer. You are furthermore the prophet of Amon and it is these prophets of the great gods of Egypt who will accompany the Pharaoh.'

On the occasion of the royal jubilee feast, too, the sanctuaries of the whole country sent their representatives and a statue of their god who participated in the ceremonies and the rejoicings: a stela of Hieraconpolis [end of the Middle Kingdom] and the mission of the minister of state Ta in the year 29 of Rameses III somewhat clarifies this custom; in addition, the jubilee temple of Boubastis has preserved a picture of these priestly delegations come to the great city of the Delta for the

Pilgrimage to the holy villages (Theban tomb)

festival of the king Osorkon. No doubt, like the good people who 'drank on this occasion more wine than during the rest of the year' [Herodotus], the religious delegations did not deprive themselves of a good time: some very explicit texts indicate that when a priest encountered another priest far from his town of origin, the event could hardly pass without rejoicing. Wine was liberally drunk with laughter and singing. . . . But the priestly reunions also allowed for the discussion of common problems concerning the various sanctuaries of the country, taxes, revenues, repairs to be made, desirable extensions; the priests could thus present their grievances to the sovereign; they received from him, in exchange, collective instruction related to the starting of new cults – the royal cults for example – or new constructions.

It is evidently from these occasional reunions that the practice of the synods arose which we see forming and developing in the time of the first Ptolemies. Every year, thereafter, a priestly assembly met in the capital, constituted itself a council, taking royal directives and discussing with high-ranking individuals of the State problems concerning the temples and priesthoods. These meetings could continue for as long as four months at times: the clergy is still a state within a state which can deal with the sovereign. In what spirit? It is easy to imagine: the Ptolemies had little but scorn for the Egyptian cults and regarded the priests with the interested eye of a breeder who sees his cattle growing fat; the clergy, on its part, coult not consider without repugnance the sad individuals who appeared in the name of the pharaohs and presented themselves

105

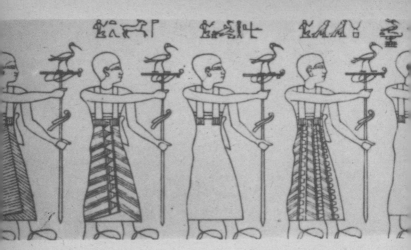

Delegation of priests (Temple of Dendereh)

in the temples as supreme actors of the divine cult. . . . But the
Ptolemies needed the clergy, which exercised a certain influence
on the masses of people, and contributed to supporting the myth
of the Macedonian-Pharaoh; the priests, in turn, gained certain
fiscal advantages, rights, immunities, by appearing loyal to their

new masters. In a climate of reciprocal scorn, the Church and the State thus often found it to their interest to give each other mutual support.

But the priestly councils had their day only once – when the Ptolemies decided it was useful (by a few concessions) to culti-

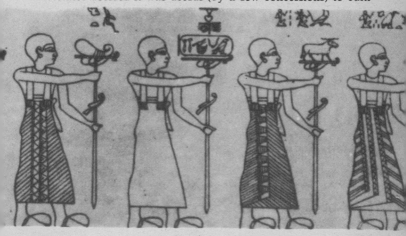

vate the favor of the Egyptian clergies. With the arrival of the Romans, everything changed, and the priests became nothing more than functionaries who were strictly watched over by a rigid administration.

Before closing this chapter dedicated to the priestly activities outside the temples, we must say a few words about a final category of 'priest' of whom there has been little to say until now: those who handled the funeral ceremonies. For lack of a special term in English, we are kept to the limits of the names 'servants of the god' and 'funerary priests.' In fact, these two categories of officiants have in common only the religious character of their offices. If it happens in effect that the priests of the dead belong to a clergy – that of the gods of the beyond, Anubis and Osiris – they are most of the time independent of the sanctuaries, and constitute a kind of professional brotherhood having absolutely nothing to do with the cult of the gods and the outside activities the priests usually performed. Only the priest-readers, because of their acquaintance with the sacred scriptures, could at the same time be counted among the temple personnel and appear at the ceremonies of the dead.

The 'funerary priests' had an important role to play at burials: they were the ones who read the ritual chapters, performing over the mummy or the statue of the dead person all the propitiatory or regenerative rites which were supposed to transform the poor human carcass, duly dried and salted by the embalmers, into a new, rejuvenated body endowed with all its former earthly faculties and likely to make a good appearance in the paradise of the beyond.

The officiants we see participating in the funerals in general bore very archaic names – those perhaps of their distant ancestors who had participated in the royal funerals in prehistoric times: *Imi Khent, chancellor of the god, companion. . . .* The general concept can still be seen: the burial ceremonies represented on the walls of the tombs reproduce, in the custom of the rich deceased of Egyptian society, rites which were once reserved for the funerals of the petty kings of the Delta: the officiants would have preserved the titles which, on these occasions, were borne by the priests or the intimates who accompanied the dead leader to his final dwelling. The details of these ceremonies would be too complex to describe here; let us say simply that they consisted of many recitations, sprinklings of water, fumigations of incense, and, at the door of the tomb, the essential rite of *the opening of the mouth,* in which one of the officiants equipped with an adze makes a gesture over the statue of parting the lips of the dead so that he may use his power of speech and various other physical faculties.

After the burial, it was necessary to insure the existence of the dead to whom feeling and appetite had been given: already the reliefs or the paintings which decorated the walls of the tomb saw to this purpose: to create, by simple representation, everything the dead could need in his life in the other world. But these drawings were, in a sense, only for extreme occasions: normally the funerary cult had to provide all the physical requirements of the dead.

A particular category of ministers, the 'servants of ka,' had as their role the daily or periodic maintenance, at the feasts of the necropolis, of the offering table and the libation altar of the dead; with their tomb, the deceased often received a little donation of land which allowed the funerary priest to live and perpetuate his cult. This 'meal,' which was served regularly to the dead, was originally the exact replica of those which were consumed by the living. With time, they became more symbolic, and were even reduced, in the lower epochs, to a simple libation of water which the *choachytes* sprinkled, reciting the ritual formula inherited from ancient times, for the greater well-being of the deceased and the enjoyment of his frail shadow wandering on the roads of the beyond.

THE SACRED WISDOM

In going through the ancient Greek texts, one cannot escape the idea that in the eyes of these old authors, Egypt was the cradle of all knowledge and all wisdom. The most celebrated among the Hellenic wise men or philosophers crossed the sea to seek, with the priests, initiation into new knowledge. And if they never went, their biographers hastened to add to the episodes of their life this voyage which had become as traditional as it was necessary.

What were these celebrated voyagers? First the great ancestors, Orpheus, who took part, in Egypt, in the feasts of the Dionysian mysteries [Diodorus I, 23, 2] and Homer himself, who visited the country [Diodorus I, 69]. In less mythical times, Solon, in his turn, crossed the sea; Plato has described his voyage:

> Solon said that the people of Sais received him very well, and in interrogating the priests wisest in these matters on the antiquities, he stated that no one among the Greeks, and he above all, knew a single word of these questions. One day, to induce the Egyptian priests to expound the antiquities, he began to relate all the most ancient things we know: Phoroneus, said to be the first man, Niobe, the flood of Deucalion and Pyrrha, with everything he had been

told about it. He gave the geneology of all their descendents; he tried, by calculating the years, to determine the date of these events. But the oldest one among the priests exclaimed: 'Solon, Solon, you Greeks are always children; there are no old men in Greece!'

'What are you trying to say?' asked Solon.

'You are young in spirit,' replied the Egyptian priest, 'for you possess no truly antique tradition, no notion gray with time. . . .'

And the old priest continued his proof: permanent catastrophes trouble the surface of the globe, mix or change the races, destroying one civilization to replace it with another; the last, far from absorbing the intellectual and scientific heritage of the one preceding it, picks up at the beginning and has to traverse again the entire lost road. But Egypt, through its geographical and climatic characteristics, avoids this almost general rule:

> For in Egypt, in any case, the waters do not rush from mountain heights but seem, on the contrary, to spring from the earth. That is why, thus spared, it is said that here are preserved the oldest traditions. . . . Thus there is nothing beautiful nor great nor remarkable done, be it in your country, or here, or in another country known to us, which has not long since been consigned to writing and preserved in our temples. [Plato, Timeus, 22-23.]

It is thus in Egypt that the Hellenic historian can find the best sources of information. But this was not the only knowledge that the priests of Egypt could impart to their foreign guests. Thus Thales of Milet made a voyage to the priests and the astronomers of Egypt, and, according to his biographers, he seems to have learned geometry from the Egyptians [Diogenes Laerce, *Thales*, 43 and 24]. Geometry and astronomy, these are the two disciplines to which the Greek authors most often refer in relation to the Egyptian priests. They sometimes add theology, when the priests agreed to reveal the mysteries to their guests – which was not often. The priests did not always receive these questioning tourists with enthusiasm; many a time they found them annoying, always indiscreet, too rigorously logical in their reasoning, occasionally sceptical, more inclined to credit faith to the reasoning of the spirit than to the fantastic stories of a thousand-year tradition. . . . Instructed by several

114

previous experiences with the intellectual tendencies of the curious Hellenes, the priests attempted to rid themselves of Pythagoras when, on the advice of Thales, he came to seek revelations of knowledge and faith among them.

Porphyrius (233-304 A.D.) recounts the voyage of Pythagoras in these terms:

> Having been received by Amasis (the king of Egypt 568-526 B.C.), he obtained from him letters of recommendation from the priests of Heliopolis, who sent him to the priests of Memphis as being older — which was, basically, nothing but a pretext. Then, from Memphis, he was sent again for the same reasons to the priests of Diospolis (Thebes). These, fearing the king and not daring to find an excuse to expel the newcomer from their sanctuary, thought to rid themselves by forcing him to submit to very bad treatment and to execute very difficult orders completely foreign to the Hellenic education. All that was thus calculated to push him to despair and finally to turn him from his undertaking. But as he executed with zeal all that was asked of him, the priests ended by conceiving a great admiration for him, treating him with respect and even allowing him to sacrifice to their gods, which had never until then been accorded to a stranger [Porphyrius, *Life of Pythagoras,* 7].

This zeal, this obstinance, this thirst for learning, ended in opening all the doors to him which were at first resolutely closed, and winning the favor of the priests. Another biographer, Jamblicus, shows us Pythagoras

> frequenting all the sanctuaries of Egypt with great ardor...., admired by the priests and soothsayers with whom he lived, instructed in everything with the greatest attention..., seeking to know personally all those who were reputed for their intelligence, not missing any religious ceremony, and visiting every country where it seemed to him he could learn something new. It is thus that he met all the priests, learning from each what he knew. And it is in these conditions that he passed twenty-two years in the temples of Egypt. [Jamblicus, *Life of Pythagoras,* 4, 18-19.]

What were the disciplines whose elements he sought? Geometry above all, for 'one finds among the Egyptians many problems in geometry ... all line theorems spring from it [Jamblicus], and astronomy, which he studied in the sanctuaries during his

115

entire stay in Egypt.' In brief, he acquired among the priests of Thebes and of Memphis 'knowledge for which he is generally considered a scholar' [Jamblicus], going as far as to secure in his own instruction the mysterious and symbolic methods which the priests were accustomed to practice [Plutarch, Isis and Osiris, 10].

Still other wise men, other Greek philosophers, came to learn in the Egyptian temples; we have occasional detail of what they derived from these stays. Oenopidus, for example, learned several secrets from priests and astronomers; in particular, that the sun has an oblique course (the ecliptic, oblique on the celestial equator), directed in a way contrary to that of the other stars [Diodorus, I, 98]. Democritus, on his part, visited the priests five years to learn things related to astronomy [Diodorus, I, 98] and geometry [Diogenes Laerce, *Democritus,* 3].

As for Plato, he seems to have sought in Egypt to learn both geometry and theology [anonymous, *Life*], and of the priestly knowledge in general [Olympiodorus, *Life of Plato*]. He must have run into the same reticence that Pythagoras had already encountered: the geographer Strabo, in his description of Egypt [XVII, I, 29] in fact speaks in these terms of his voyage to Heliopolis:

> We saw there the buildings dedicated formerly to the lodging of priests; but this is not all: we were shown also the dwelling of Plato and of Eudoxus; for Eudoxus accompanied Plato this far: arrived at Heliopolis, they established themselves here and both resided there thirteen years in the society of the priests: the fact is affirmed by several authors. These priests, so profoundly versed in the knowledge of celestial phenomena, were at the same time mysterious people, seldom communicative, and it was only due to time and adroit management that Eudoxus and Plato were able to be initiated by them into several of their theoretical speculations. But these barbarians retained the best part in their own possession. And if the world today owes to them its knowledge of how many fractions of the day (from the entire day) must be added to the full 365 days to have a complete year, the Greeks were ignorant of the true length of the year and many other facts of the same nature until translations in Greek of the Memoirs of the Egyptian priests spread these notions among the modern astronomers, who have continued up to now to draw largely from this same source as in the writings and observations of the Chaldeans.

Eudoxus was nevertheless recommended by Agesilas to Nectanebo, king of Egypt, who presented him to the priests; in the course of his stay, he had to content himself nevertheless with imploring instruction from the Heliopolitan priests, inasmuch as Plutarch informs us, on his part, that Eudoxus followed the lessons of Chonouphis of Memphis [Isis and Osiris, 10]. Perhaps, as was already the case in the time of the king Amasis, the priests of Heliopolis had slyly passed him into the good care of the clergy of Memphis, 'older and – hence – more learned than they.' However it was, Euxodus made the best of this stay, as tradition attributes to him the translation into Greek of written works in Egyptian [Diogenes Laerce] and the introduction into his country of exact notions on the course of the five planets, up till then poorly determined, and whose real nature he had learned in Egypt [Seneca, Quaest. Nat., VII, 3] – no doubt the 'theory of the epicycles.'

What were these witnesses worth? Let us guard against being too credulous: a good part of the citations reported above is the work of later biographers, in whose eyes the Egyptian voyage constituted an indispensable episode in the life of their philosophers – a little like the doctorate years that the African and Asian students come to spend in European universities. Egypt was thus considered the country of the sciences; it became desirable that all the old sages should have had a stay there. At least the tradition succeeded in affirming this, even if certain of them never actually placed a foot there.

Nevertheless it is not to describe some vague spiritual heritage, not to emphasize what 'Greece owes to Egypt,' that we have recalled these voyages of the philosophers. Nor is it to establish, after the classic sources, the places where Egyptian science was developed: the voyagers informed themselves on what interested them, no more, and we will see later that besides geometry and astronomy, theology and history, the Egyptian priests cultivated a host of other disciplines of which our tourists say nothing. These several citations have revealed to us a fact more important in itself than the historical reality of these voyages: the general renown of the wisdom and knowledge which excited the Greeks of antiquity found in the priestly schoolroom of the great Egyptian sanctuaries. There is an added point: the philosophers of Greece, as celebrated as they were, won still more popular admiration when one could find an Egyptian sojourn at the source of their knowledge.

Secondly, we know now, thanks to the Greeks, a few traits, a few aspects of the priestly science: its secret character, and the reluctance the priests felt in divulging its elements; the symbolism and the mystery which surrounded the revelations they allowed themselves to impart. Finally we know the place an unlimited faith occupied in the elaboration of this wisdom in the disclosures of the written texts and in the literary tradition of the past.

SPIRIT AND CHARACTERISTICS OF THE SACRED WISDOM

With this wealth of predominant ideas, we can now turn to the Egyptian sources, and attempt to define the 'spiritual climate' in which the priestly wisdom operated. A simple review of the areas it covers would be in fact insufficient to bring out the specific characteristics which distinguished it from a 'lay' course of research – and which powerfully influenced its nature and its success. This wisdom was progressively built up by living men in a world fundamentally oriented to religious problems – theology – and the exercise of the cult. It is therefore of practical design – but practical in the framework of a given spiritual system; it is also *traditional,* hostile to innovations. In short it implies, basically, the *knowledge of a body of writing* which gives access to the ancient texts, permanent source of all revelation, but also gives rise to a particular mode of thought, based on the divine worth of the articulations of the language and the expressive possibilities – almost unlimited – of the hieroglyphs. Looking to the old texts, faith in the omnipotence of sounds, progressive specialization in the hieroglyphic literature for religious use, and pursuit, in this writing, of a manifold mode of expression, such are the underlying elements which conditioned the 'priestly wisdom,' and conferred on it its original outlook.

THE OBSESSION WITH THE WRITTEN WORD

In every age, it appears that the Egyptians were haunted by the idea of finding the elements of a 'lost' truth in the old parchments. This tendency they owed to the paper-ridden character of their civilization; but something deeper than this one factor – this single scribbling vice – must be added.

To understand the attitude of the Egyptians, it is necessary to emphasize the striking contrast between their view of the world and ours. We live in a universe which we know is in perpetual movement: each new problem demands a new solution. But for the Egyptians, this notion of time which modifies the current knowledge of the world, of an alteration of factors which forces a change in methods, had no place. In the beginning, the divinity created a stable world, fixed, definitive; this world *functions*, as a motor well oiled and well fed; if there are 'misfires,' if the motor fades, if one of the parts making it up is worn out or broken, it is replaced and everything starts off again even better than before. But this motor would always remain the same, its mechanism, its appearance, its output, would always be identical. . . . If some problem intrigues the mind, therefore, if some serious event arises to disturb the customary order of thing it could not be *really* new: it was foreseen with the world, its solution or its remedy exists in all eternity, revealed in a kind of universal 'manner of use,' that the gods defined in creating the universe itself. What is necessary, then, is to find in the ancient writings the formula that foresaw such and such a case. . . . Before a given event, a physical phenomenon, a catastrophe striking the whole country, the scholar would not seek to discover the actual causes in order to find an appropriate remedy: he would examine with scholarly ardor the volumes of old writings to find out if the event had already occurred in some moment of the past, and what solution was then applied to it. . . .

Nothing is more characteristic, on this subject, than the story of the great famine which struck Egypt under a Ptolemy, and which has been transmitted to us by a stela engraved on a rock on the isle of Seheil.

The Nile had not risen for seven years. The grain was no longer abundant, the seeds were dry, everything that could be eaten was sparse, everyone was disappointed in his income. People no longer had the strength to walk; children were in tears; young men were defeated; the old ones had a sad heart. They were seated on the ground, their legs folded, their hands against them; even the courtesans were in need; and the temples were closed, the sanctuaries were dusty; in short all that existed was in distress.

What was to be done at this point? Revise the system of interior distribution or import wheat? Improve the irrigation system? Not at all. If the Nile did not flood at the proper time, there was something wrong at Elephantine, in the divine conditions which regulated the flood; and the priest sought it in the old papers:

> Then, says the king, I resolved to turn to the past and I asked a priest (. . .) about Imhotep. . . : 'Where does the Nile rise? What town of the winding river is there? What god rests there to assist

The Isle of Elephantine

me?' He rises: 'I am going to the city of Thoth, I will enter the room of the archives, I will unroll the holy books, and I will take guidance from them,' Then he went, and returned to me in an instant, letting me know the course of the Nile (in the regions of the cataract) and of everything with which they are provided. He revealed to me marvelous and mysterious things; ancestors went there, but no king has gone here since the beginning of time.

And the text goes on: the king discovers that the god Khnum presides over these regions; he conciliates him with offerings, gives him a gift of land, and everything returns to order. . . .

Thus the quest for the old magic books is one of the frequent themes in Egyptian literature – the final recourse of scholars in trouble. . . . Sometimes it is only a question of a lost document, which a favored scribe finds by chance: the contents seem interesting to him, and he copies them out for use.

This is how we possess, in the vast collection of religious and magic formulas known by the name of *Book of the Dead,* a section with the impressive title: 'Formula to stop the heart of the deceased as he is transported to the Other World.' This precious document, reproduced on papyrus hundreds of times, was found under special circumstances described as follows:

> This formula was found at Hermopolis on a tablet of basalt from the South, inscribed with true lapis, under the feet of the Majesty of King Mycerinos, by the son of the King Djedefhor, true of voice. He found it when he was moving to make inventories in the temples. As he was put to trouble for this, he asked for it in compensation, and brought it back as a marvel to the king.

Another document of great importance, the magic stela 'Metternich,' was drawn up under similar circumstances: a priest by the name of Estatoum, in the time of the king Nectanebo II (359-341 B.C.), the last sovereign of Egypt, stated that an important inscription had been found in the temple of Osiris-Mnevis at Heliopolis. Interested in this text and wishing to please the god, he had it copied, then transcribed on a magnificent stela of dark green stone.

As to the great temple of the goddess Hathor at Dendereh, which was rebuilt under the last Ptolemies, a text from the crypts specifies that its general location was inspired by a very old document.

121

The God Thoth (Temple of Edfu)

The venerable establishment in Dendereh has been found in the ancient writings, writings on a leather scroll in the time of the ministers of Horus [the sovereigns before Menes], found at Memphis in a casket of the royal palace, in the time of the king of Upper and Lower Egypt, Lord of the Two Countries. . . Pepi.

The Greco-Roman temple was suggested then by orders as old as 3000 years, found 2600 years later by a prying archivist in an old box of papers. . . .

Antiquity could already confer an appreciable value on the writings; but there were among the privileged texts certain priceless ones were worth risking one's life to recover. A popular story of the low epoch, which comes to us by a papyrus written in *demotic*, tells us, for example, about the misadventures of the royal son Nenoferkaptah in quest of a book written in the hand of the god Thoth. . . .

Nenoferkaptah seemed to be on earth only to walk in the city of the dead of Memphis [the plateau of Saqqara], reciting the writings which are in the tombs of the Pharaohs and the stelae of the scribes of the House of Life, as well as the inscriptions which cover them, for he was impassioned to the extreme by writings. Then a procession in honor of Ptah took place, and Nenoferkaptah entered the temple to pray. However, as he followed the procession, furtively reading the writings which covered the chapels of the gods, an old man saw him and began to laugh. Nenoferkaptah said to him: 'Why are you laughing at me?' The priest said to him: 'It is not at you I am laughing; but can I help laughing when you are reading here the writings which are worthless? If you really want to read a writing, come with me, I will take you to a place where there is a book which Thoth wrote by hand, himself, when he descended to earth behind the gods. Two formulas are written there. If you read the first, you will charm the sky, the earth, the world of the night, the mountains, the waters; you will understand what the birds of the sky and the reptiles say, every one of them; you will see the fish of the lowest depths, for a divine force hovers above them on the water. If you read the second formula, even if you are in the tomb, you will resume the form you had on earth; you will even see the sun rising to the sky with his following of gods, and the moon in the form that she takes to appear. . . .'

But this invaluable magic book is not the easiest to find: by dint of favors, the son of the king persuades the old priest to speak, and the latter reveals the hiding place to him.

This book is in the middle of the sea of Koptos, in a casket of iron; the iron casket contains a casket of bronze; the casket of bronze contains a casket of cinnamon wood; the casket of cinnamon wood contains a casket of ivory and ebony; the casket of ivory and ebony contains a casket of silver; the casket of silver contains a casket of gold, and the book is in this. And there is a nest of serpents, scorpions, and reptiles of all sorts around the casket in which the book lies, and there is an immortal serpent wound around the casket in question. . . .

Nenoferkaptah ended by recovering this exceptional book. The reading of the formulas produced the desired effect, but Thoth considered himself aggrieved, and the imprudent one paid for his curiosity with his life and with those of all his kinsmen.

With time however the god became less easily offended. A more recent story than the one we have mentioned, which deals with the same hero, reports an episode of magic competitions between the sovereigns of Egypt and of Meroë. Each magician in turn defied his adversary, and at the moment where the text interests us directly, Egypt was on the losing side; every

night the Meroitic sorceror inflicted a volley of blows on the Pharaoh with sticks that left him utterly exhausted. . . . In despair, the Egyptian magician went to Hermopolis and asked assistance of the god Thoth.

> Horus, son of Panishi, lay in the temple, and he had a dream that same night. The figure of the great god Thoth spoke to him, saying: '. . . Tomorrow morning, enter the rooms of books of the temple of Hermopolis; you will find there a naos closed and sealed; you will open it, and you will find a box which contains a book, which I wrote with my own hand. Take it out, make a copy of it, then return it to its place, for it is the magic book which protects me against evils, and it is this which will protect the Pharaoh, it is this which will save him from the sorceries of the Meroitics.'

Thanks to the effectiveness of the divine book, it is the king of the Ethiopians who is beaten the following night, and Egypt triumphs. . . .

If we linger a little over these quotations, it is because they convey, in their picturesque variety, one of the characteristics closest to the Egyptian thinkers – one of the errors perhaps most disastrous to their spiritual life: the irrational faith in the omnipotence of the old texts. The quest for the old writings in fact by far surpasses the simple preoccupation of a mind curious about the past, or even of a traditional attachment to old methods of thought or action. It reveals in fact the conviction that invaluable secrets are hidden, forgotten, lost, in the dusty archives – secrets not only useful for the advice they can give, but actually all-powerful, able to render, to the one who discovers them, a means of irresistible action over universal forces. The sacred archives transmitted not only the memory of old events, or the curious episodes of the past: they could, in special cases, reveal the same words which had once served the gods in creating the universe. . . .

THE OMNIPOTENCE OF SOUNDS AND SACRED ETYMOLOGY

The creation of the world was pictured, by the Egyptians, in various ways; each city conceived it in its own way, but left, as is logical, the principal part to its local god. A 'technical' creator seems however to have been similar in all the theologies and the agent was the *word*. The initial god, to create, had only to *speak*; and the beings or things evoked came from his voice. The word is not in fact, in the Egyptian spirit, a simple social tool facilitating human relationships, it is the audible expression of the deepest essence of things; it remains what it was at the beginning of the world, a divine act which gave life to matter; in the articulation of the syllables resides the secret of the existence of the things evoked: to pronounce a word, a name, is not only a technique creating in the mind of the hearer the picture which haunts that of the speaker, it is to act on the thing or being mentioned, it is to repeat the initial act of the creator. . . . When we read, in the funerary texts, that a deceased one wishes his name to be pronounced; when he begs that the formula of the offering be read in a loud voice: 'a thousand breads, a thousand pitchers of beer . . . for so-and-so,' it is not a vain appeal; in the spirit of the Egyptians, the pious visitor who reads this formula will call up, by the sound of his voice, the actual existence of whatever he calls forth, and the dead will benefit. One conceives the colossal power that a magic or sacred text could contain, the means for unlimited action that it could offer its possessor; one understands how the Egyptians gave to their sacred old archives the name of *baou-Re*, 'omnipotence of Re,' for, through these, they found the elemental force which, according to general tradition, the god Re had put into operation in the creation of the universe. . . .

Many theological facts are explained as soon as one becomes aware of this particular perspective. For example, the permanence, during a good two thousand years, of an unvarying liturgical language, corresponding to Middle Egyptian, from which the popular language departed more and more. One could not alter the sounds and grammatical forms of a language divine in its origin. Is not the Egyptian name for hieroglyphics 'divine words'? What is more eloquent, in this regard, than this passage of the hermetic writings [tract XVI, 1–2] condemning the translation of sacred works?

Hermes, my master, in the frequent conversations that he had with me. . . used to tell me that those who read my books found their composition very simple and clear, even when, on the contrary, it is obscure and hides the meaning of the words, and it will become even more obscure when the Greeks, later, will get it into their heads to translate from our language to theirs, which will end in a complete distortion of the text and in full obscurity. By contrast, expressed in the original language, this discourse preserves in full clarity the sense of the words: and in fact even the particularity of sound and the proper intonation of Egyptian terms retain in themselves the force of things said.

Never did the Egyptians consider the language – that corresponding to the hieroglyphics – as a *social* instrument; it always remained for them the sonorous echo of the basic energy which sustains the universe, a *cosmic force*. Thus the study of this language gave them an 'explanation' of the world.

This explanation is provided for them by a 'game of words.' From the moment one considers words as intimately connected

Scene from the myth of Horus (Temple of Edfu)

with the essence of beings or things that they define, similarities of terms are no longer accidental: they convey a relationship in nature, a subtle rapport that the wisdom of the priests would have to define: names of places, names of divinities, terms designating sacred objects, all become explicable through a phonetic etymology – and the door is open to the most extravagant fantasies. . . .

Thus we see some classic examples of this technique, infallible in their eyes, beginning with those of the 'Myth of Horus.' It concerns a vast mythological composition, sometimes appearing in the form of a 'drama,' which might be played in successive episodes. This text, composed at the occasion of the fourth great annual feast of the god Horus of Edfu, the 'feast of victory,' relates the exploits of Re and Horus, who came down from the Upper Nile sailing in triumph, scattering before them all the evil spirits, all the associates of the god of evil. The story progresses geographically, from South to North, and the idea of the writer is to explain each of the names of the towns that the god passed through in his voyage by one of his actions or one of his words.

> Horus says then: 'Come, O Re, to see how your enemies have fallen before you in this country.' And His Majesty comes, accompanied by Astarte. He sees that the enemies have fallen to earth, with heads shattered. Re says then to Horus: 'This is a pleasant place to live' [*nedjem ankh pou*], and for this reason the palace of Horus Nedjemankh is thus called to this day. And Re says to Thoth: 'Thus my enemies are punished' [*djeba*], and for this reason this nome is called Dejbou [Edfu] to this day. . . .

Thus each city, each place-name, takes a definite role in the movement of the great god – and receives an etymology that can make the hair of the linguists grow gray. There is for example an establishment of the Ancient Kingdom, in Upper Egypt, in the vicinity of the town of Esna, which carries the name of Pi-Sahura, 'the domain of the king Sahura.' Its presence, close to a second town by the name of Hout-Snefrou, 'the castle of the king Snefrou,' 'Castelsnefrou,' shows that this area was, under the kings of the fourth and fifth dynasties (around 2700–2600 B.C.) in the time of the pyramids, a rich country where agriculture flourished. However, this name of Pi-Sahura was understood quite differently in the low epoch;

it was translated: 'the house where the god Re stayed (sahu),' and the establishment of this little town was thus related to an episode of the divine wanderings. . . . All the historical interest of this toponymy becomes, by this fact, lost.

This process may appear infantile and not very serious. It is logical nevertheless if we try to understand the value the Egyptians attached to the articulations of words: every external resemblance between two terms had to convey a direct relationship between the two elements evoked. Thus it became a general practice, used in every epoch, introduced into every area, becoming, in the priestly science, the essential procedure for explaining proper names – practically the definition itself of the nature of the gods. . . . So it was of the god Amon, the great patron of Thebes. What his name means exactly, we do not know. It is pronounced in the same way as another word which means 'to hide,' 'hide oneself,' and the scribes played on this similarity to define Amon as the great god who masks his real aspect from his children. . . . But some did not hesitate to go even further: Hecate of Abderus gave credence to a priestly tradition according to which the name (Amon) was the term used in Egypt to call someone. . . . It is true that the word *amoini* means 'come,' 'come to me'; it is a fact, on the other hand, that certain hymns begin with the words *Amoini A-moun*. . . . 'Come to me, Amon.' The singular similarity of these two words aroused the priests to suspect some intimate relation between them – and to find the explanation for the divine name: 'thus, addressing themselves to the primordial god . . . as to a being invisible and hidden, they invited and exhorted him, calling him Amon, to show and reveal himself to them.'

Highest powers credited to the old magic books, faith in the creative quality of sounds, in the original divinity of language, explicative value of the 'popular' etymologies, these are three essential characteristics of Egyptian priestly thought, three screens through which all knowledge appeared to them. Let us add the knowledge of the hieroglyphics, with all the evocative richness which this system of writing implies, and we will have an adequate perception of the 'intellectual climate' in which, century after century, the 'sacred wisdom' was worked out.

THE MYSTERIES OF THE HIEROGLYPHICS

Writing appeared in Egypt around the year 3000; the last

129

One of the last hieroglyphic texts

hieroglyphic text that we have discovered is dated the twenty-fourth of August 394 A.D.; between the first important text in Egyptian and this last graphic manifestation in the time of Theodosius, there are hardly any more grammatical divergences than between a text of Terence and a thesis written at the Sorbonne in terms of 'syntax,' 'phraseology,' and the dictionary. However during the same period, the *spoken* language was modified in such proportions that an Egyptian of the Ancient Kingdom would be as much at ease before a coptic text as Virgil before a novel of the 'black series' (or, one might say, 'before a modern novel'). . . . It is a normal phenomenon: nothing can arrest the evolution of a *spoken* language, especially when there are no schools, printers, books in great profusion, which could contribute to stabilizing it – at least slowing down its natural course. But one can imagine that a clergy held it important to maintain unchanged a language whose sounds were the creative agents of the world, and whose writing was of divine origin. . . . Are not the religious services in the Catholic churches of the whole world performed in Latin, as in the time of the first Christians?

Drawing on a special body of writing, unchanging in its prin-

Wood panel of Hesi (around 2900)

131

ciples and set in its vocabulary, the priestly circles then applied themselves to keeping alive among themselves the knowledge and the practice; they wanted also to be able to refine, to elaborate from this the whole system of sacred etymology, to develop its resources by carrying to an absurd extreme the principles which would define its meanings. Thus one witnesses in the last periods of Egyptian civilization an astonishing multiplication in the number of symbols: during the classic periods, Middle and New Kingdoms, around 600 hieroglyphics sufficed to fill all the needs of writers. Now the scribes multiplied the variations, created new symbols, revived archaic forms. . . . The press of the French Institute of Oriental Archaeology, the best-equiped· in the world, has more than 6000 hieroglyphic characters: nevertheless on the publication of each new text of the low epoch, some characters must be delineated which were not known before. . . . Elsewhere the sacred writers, in exploiting the principles which always governed the endowment of a certain phonetic value to each hieroglyph, started to multiply these values. A symbol which could only be read in one way now acquired two, three, four or five supplementary values. . . . The scribes of the temples played with their writing, multiplying its resources and making an instrument infinitely subtle and complicated, developing it to infinity, unaware of its overwhelming difficulty; on the contrary, aware of the almost unlimited possibilities that the gods had thus put into their hands. We witness a veritable crisis of growth, of which writing is the victim; it attained a disquieting proliferation. We imagine the scholars overjoyed at having found new symbols, at having conceived some new value, and proud to suggest these findings to their colleagues. . . . They reread the old texts in quest of older forms, they compete in ingenuity to contrive new meanings, they play on their virtuosity, and this game leads to ever new discoveries. . . .

GAME OF SYMBOLS AND PHILOSOPHY OF WRITING

Satisfied to have written a traditional phrase by using unusual symbols, the scribe is suddenly brought up short: the sense of the text comes from the phonetic value of the symbols used; but these symbols themselves, by their physical aspect alone, call forth certain ideas independent of their phonetic value: let us write, for example, the name of the god Ptah, the divine patron of the city of Memphis, using the original symbols.

P will be drawn as the sky (;(t)); *t* as the earth (ta), *h* as the figure of the god *Heh* with raised arms. However, in the Memphis theology, one of the functions attributed to the god Ptah is that of having, in the beginning, separated the heaven from the earth. In putting the god Heh between the sky (p) that he supports and the earth (t) that he tramples underfoot, one thus grasps at the same time the phonetic orthography of the divine name Ptah, and a little scene which *visually* evokes the functions attributed to this god. . . . Let us write yet another word which designates the world of the dead, the douat. It is spelled, at this time, *d + t*, the same as the word for 'body,' and also for 'eternity.' In combining the symbol of the serpent (*d*) and that of the prone mummy (*wt*), one thus phonetically obtains the sound 'douat,' while calling forth the other world by the image of the dead body circled by the coils of the guardian serpent of hell. . . . It is now a new game for the scribes to choose, in the unlimited arsenal of symbols having the same meaning, those which could (their basic goal) convey the necessary sounds in pronouncing a word and permit, by their grouping, suggestive little scenes related to the idea expressed: the text thus speaks doubly, to the spirit which follows the words, and to the eyes which perceive the images – a little like a film where the subtitles describe the action represented (two men fight; subtitle: they fight). . . .

Finally, in the last stage of these wide experimentations with hieroglyphic writing, the scholar-priests came to conceive, in relation to the symbols of their religious texts, the possibility of formal speculations somewhat analogous to the cabalist research on the Hebrew alphabet. If this writing of divine origin, whose very articulations were generators of life, could at the same time establish and transmit an idea expressed through sounds, and suggest this idea by the graphic image, was it not possible to imagine an orthography even richer with ideas than the name written? Could not the drawing surpass in meaning the phonetic expression? In place of simply confirming, by a visual scene, the idea which would evoke the word pronounced, the spelling of a divine name would henceforth create around this name an *aura* of secondary ideas, a whole series of descriptive adjectives which could be applied, in the context, to this divinity.

Let us take an example: the picture for the name of Neith,

133

the primordial goddess, whose name is written in Egyptian by
means of the two consonants N and t. One sometimes finds, to
express this, the picture ⸻⸻ the vulture equalling N,
the sun t; but each of these two symbols can
have other meanings, more often, the first
serving as the written *mwt*, 'mother,' the second, Re, 'sun'; the
text here calls for the phonetic reading 'Neith,' but, in view
of the symbols, a richer parallel translation asserts itself: 'the
mother of the Re,' an idea that the scribe wished to suggest,
for the text continues in these terms: '(Neith), the mother of
the unique god who has no equal (Re).' The functions, the
possible adjectives for a god, existed thus in a latent state in
the *phonetic* spelling (whose symbols have been carefully chosen)
of his name. Another example, relating to the same divine
name: Neith can be written ⸻⸻ $N + t$; but the first part
is the ruffled surface of the water, which enters into
the word *nt,* watery surface; ⸻⸻ and the second is the symbol designating the earth, *ta*: the text continues: '(Neith), the
primeval water which gave birth to the land.' Here again, the
spelling of the divine name already evokes, by its appearance,
the descriptions of the goddess which the text goes on to attribute
to her. . . .

Usually these last speculations can only be verified in the
very lowest epoch: we discover something of it in the religious
texts of the temple of Esna, which date from the emperors
Domitian and Trajan – of the first two centuries of our era.
They show to what point the study of hieroglyphic writing had
been advanced by the priestly groups until the last decades of
its use. Less than ever before did the priests consider hieroglyphs
as simple orthographic tools: they had practically come to make
them a mode of triple expression, able at will (and sometimes
simultaneously) to serve as *letters* (phonetic elements constituting
a word), to design *scenes* parallel to the idea expressed, doubling
the auditory perception by a visual awareness, and even *to
suggest in advance,* beyond the word that it serves to spell, the
adjectives and functions with which the word might ultimately
be endowed. . . . No doubt from simple drawing games the sacred
scribes came to realize that the rich writing at their disposition
allowed, beyond its immediate use as a means of expression,
a definition of the world which was at the same time visual
and symbolic: the universe, its laws and its history, were born
from the pronunciation of the divine words: a part of this secret

force, of this all-powerful primeval energy, remained enclosed in the secret of their hieroglyphs.

After these several insights into the intellectual climate in which the sacred wisdom developed, one can imagine that the priests did not willingly reveal it: how could they present simply to a stranger – almost a tourist – the diverse branches of a body of knowledge whose fundamentals were so closely tied to the basic religious ideas of Egypt? How could they offer, in a clear picture, the sum of ideas and convictions to which they had only come themselves through laborious meditation, through the accumulation, generation after generation, of sacred traditions, writings, spiritual techniques? The knowledge of a sacred language and its writings, the assiduous study of the old texts, the constant awareness of the unlimited power of its sounds and words, such were the basic conditions of the whole sacred wisdom; such were, in the eyes of the Egyptian priests, the only steps which allowed access to it.

The spirit of this wisdom being thus defined, what positive data do we possess on it? Where was it distributed? What areas did it cover?

HOUSES OF LIFE AND LIBRARIES OF TEMPLES

We will find an initial response to these questions by examining what we know of the Houses of Life and the Libraries of Temples.

The Houses of Life are institutions still rather mysterious to us. The Egyptians spoke of them without giving details. We know for certain that they existed at Memphis, Abydos, El Amarna, Akhmim, Coptos, Esna and Edfu – and we suppose that each fairly important temple possessed, as an annex, its House of Life. These structures were rather like the offices where the sacred wisdom was developed, where the texts were studied, copied, assembled; perhaps some instruction was given there – at least we know of a professor of the House of Life of Abydos, and we know, thanks to the story of Satni, that the infant Senosiris, with little instruction in the elements of Egyptian writing, was assigned a scribe and set to reading the magic books with the scribes of the House of Life of the temple of Ptah. It is possible that the young man simply associated with professional scribes to train himself, or even – which would conform to the general tone of the story – to dazzle them with his already superhuman knowledge. . . .

The main activities of the House of Life consisted in preparing the religious works necessary to the cult, in recopying the old manuscripts, in correcting errors, in completing the gaps and passages short of lines; they developed the texts of theology or of liturgy particular to each temple; they prepared the magic books of protection, the astronomical tables; they recopied, a thousand times, versions of the Book of the Dead; they discussed with ardor, between copying sessions, philosophical and religious problems, without neglecting medicine and literary activities. . . . For everything was not just mechanical copying, in these studies; sometimes an original text, sometimes a theological exposition would be drawn up following meditation or the exchange of fruitful views. . . . Some of the finest spiritual or ethical texts we possess were stimulated by the reflections and convictions of some obscure scribe whose name will never be known to us. . . .

Besides these scribes, the Houses of Life also included several specialists: *the ritual executor,* for example, who was charged, in magic ceremonies, with striking the accursed animals according to a defined ritual; and also the entire group of *artists* and *decorators,* who had to cover the walls of the temples with

Chester-Beatty papyrus before unrolling

Funerary papyrus

inscriptions and reliefs, to paint the hieroglyphs and the scenery, to repair sections of the walls and texts which might be damaged.

One can, in short, conclude that all that was written on the walls of the temples, like all the papyri necessary to the cult, as well as all the elements of the priestly culture, came from the Houses of Life. What these elements were, the lists of the Libraries of Temples will reveal to us.

If the scribes of the Houses of Life prepared the rough drafts of the texts which the sculptors cut into the temple walls or preserved in their archives the originals of the most important theological texts, they were also called on to write out the scrolls necessary to the priests for the performance of the daily ritual. These papyri were preserved in the same temple, ready to be used. On many of them, in small sections and generally rather obscure, the name 'House of Books' has been found. Narrow niches dug into the thickness of the walls formerly contained these scrolls. A sort of inventory of works deposited in these rooms was engraved on the wall. Here, for example, is the list of sacred books from the temple of Edfu:

The books and the great parchments of pure leather, enabling
    the beating of the devil;
    the repulsion of the crocodile;
    the favoring of the hour;
    the preservation of a ship;
    the promenade of the great ship;
the book for launching the king on procession;
the book for the conduct of the cult; ...
the protection of the city, of the house, of the white crown of the
    throne, of the year; ...
the book to appease Sekhmet; ...
the book for hunting the lion, repelling the crocodiles, ... driving
    off reptiles;
    knowing the secrets of the laboratory;
    knowing the divine offerings in all their detail... and all the
    inventories of the secret forms of the god, and of all the aspects
    of the associated gods, copied daily for [the] temple, every day,
    one after the other, for the 'souls' of the gods dwell in [this]
    place, and do not stray from [this] temple, ever.
the book of the temple inventory;
the book of the capture [of enemies];
the book of all writings of combat;
the book of temple regulations;
the books of guards of the temple;
instructions for the decoration of a wall;
protection of the body;
the book of magic protection of the king in his palace;
formulas for repulsing the evil eye;
knowledge of the periodical return of two stars [sun and moon];
control of the periodical return of the [other] stars;
enumeration of all the places [sacred], and knowledge of what is
    there;
all ritual relating to the exodus of the god from his temple on feast
    days. [Edfu III, 347 and 351.)

In another temple of Upper Egypt, that of Tod, several blocks

138

still bear the remainder of a similar inventory. Books found there treat of the entrance of the god Montou at Thebes, of the ritual for making up the eye of Horus, a book of offerings on the altar; from the temple of Amon, a book of the feast of Thoth; from the temple of Khons, a ritual of the feast of victory, a ritual for the birth of the god, etc. On the island of Philae, in the Roman temple of Esna, similar libraries have been found, where once the sacred literature of current usage was preserved.

Excavations have revealed works from one of these libraries in the little town of Tebtunis, at the Fayoum; among these documents, beside the rituals and treatises on astronomy and medicine, a certain number of literary texts (demotic stories of Satni and of Petoubastis), three collections of words classed according to feeling – which we designate by the term onomastic – and several already known copies of a book of wisdom have been identified.

THE DOMAINS OF THE SACRED WISDOM

If we add together the areas where the priestly wisdom had occasion to be exercised, we would arrive, thanks to these lists preserved by accident, at an astonishing picture. It is obvious that *each* priest was not equally competent in all the disciplines we have mentioned, whether among the scribes in the House of Life or in the inventories of the libraries: there was specialization; one officiant had to concern himself only with liturgy, another only with astronomy and the calculation of weather; still another with the interpretation of dreams, or with the cult of the sacred animals. . . . Nothing gives a more complete idea of this strict division of knowledge and techniques among the various categories of religions than the passage in which the Christian writer Clement of Alexandria describes the procession of the god Osiris, as it was organized in the great Hellenistic city:

At the head comes a singer, carrying a musical instrument; they say he has to know two books of Hermes, one containing the hymns to the gods, the other the royal biography. Behind him comes the soothsayer, holding in his hand his insignia, the clock and the astronomical palm. He has to know by heart the four astrological books of Hermes, one of which treats of the order of the fixed stars, the second of the movements of the sun and the moon and the five planets, the third of the encounters and illumi-

139

nations of the sun and the moon, the last of the risings of the stars. Then comes the hierogrammate coiffed with feathers, with a book in hand and the small palette in which he keeps the black ink and the calam which he uses for writing. This personage has to know the writings which are called hieroglyphics, concerning cosmography and geography, the path of the sun, of the moon and the five planets, the topography of Egypt and the description of the Nile, the prescriptions relating to sacred objects, to the places which are dedicated to them, the measures and the utensils used in the ritual. Behind, comes the stolist who carries the arm of justice and the vase of libation; he knows everything relating to the instruction of what is called 'moschosphragistical,' knowledge of the marks of animals, and the ten precepts which relate to the veneration of the gods in the country, which includes: Egyptian piety, treaties on fumigations, offerings, hymns, prayers, processions, feasts, etc. Last comes the prophet, holding the hydria conspicuously against his chest, followed by those who carry up the offerings as they are invoked. In his capacity of chief of the temple, he knows the ten books which are called hieratic thoroughly, and comprehends the totality of the priestly wisdom on the subject of the laws and the gods.

Certainly this is a rich view of the body of priestly knowledge. Some of its elements recall what we already know through the lists of the temples; others are new and add a notable supplement to the picture we would like to evoke of the sacred wisdom.

This information is nevertheless incomplete; an appreciable number of names, dispersed through the Egyptian documents, several allusions in the texts, certain rediscovered works, allow us to have a greater idea of the areas covered by the knowledge of the Egyptian priests. These scattered facts we will regroup and classify, to present as detailed a picture of the priestly spheres as possible. Let us begin with history. . . .

HISTORY

We recall the sentence of the old priest of Sais speaking to Solon: 'Nothing beautiful, or great, or remarkable, whatever it may be, has been done, in your country [Greece] or here, or in any other country known to us, which has not long since been consigned to writing and preserved in our temples.' It is in the temples that the only documents which could pass for historical essays were developed.

Egypt never had a genuine historian; this is a plain fact which must be accepted. The absence of a continuous sense of time made an exact evaluation difficult; each new king mounted the throne in the year 1; when he died, the year 1 of his successor began the same day of his accession to the throne; if one takes into account the co-regencies, parallel royalties, fictitious reigns, one can understand that an exact computation of past centuries was nearly impossible. They said, 'in the time of the king Cheops,' a little as we speak of the 'good King Alfred,' aware of a distant event but situated in time in a rather vague way. Furthermore, the idea the Egyptians had of an eternal and immutable world hindered the conception of a possible evolution in political or social conditions. There were considerable social uprisings, such as marked the end of the Ancient Kingdom. But it is the literary texts which mention them, the historical texts confine themselves to enumerating the kings who lived – by the scores – in those troubled times, without even leaving one to guess that something important could be occurring at the same time. . . . These two factors: imprecision of dates, exclusive preoccupation with the annalistic and with royal lists, weighed down for more than thirty centuries the notations of historical facts in Egypt. One must look to Manethon – a Hellenized priest – for the first book of 'history' to appear, at the price of such labor – and of such errors! . . .

We have seen no trace of an historical work in the lists of sacred books mentioned above. There were some, nevertheless, and they have reached us. Herodotus reports that the priests 'after Menes, the first king of Egypt, read from a book the names of 330 other kings; in the course of so many human generations, there were eighteen Ethiopians, and one woman – a native woman. The others were men and Egyptians.' Several lists of this kind have come down to us. One of them decorates a corridor in the temple of Abydos. The king Sethi, father of the great Rameses, is seen making the offering to 'all' his ancestors, some seventy-six kings, since Menes, the founder of Egyptian unity. More than as an historical document, it must be seen as a political document: Sethi belongs to a new dynasty, somewhat of an intruder; in attaching to himself this long line of deceased Pharaohs, he no doubt hopes to see himself recognized as legitimate. . . . Other lists, however, are undoubtedly more identifiable with what we understand to be 'historical texts'; the royal papyrus of Turin, for example, which enumerates the dynasties,

Royal list of Abydos

the kings, the length of their rule, and totals the duration of certain periods. And a document of the first dynasties, the rock of Palermo, unfortunately very mutilated, presented, reign by reign, all the important events that Egypt had known: height of the flood, date of the death of each king and coronation of his successor, voyages by sea, commercial or military undertakings. . . . To these official notations, the priestly annals add astronomical observations, and miracles. . . .

'Thus,' says Herodotus, 'there are 11,340 years during which the priests told me that no god had appeared in human form. . . . However, they informed me that four times during this period the sun rose at a point in the sky which was not its own; and that twice it rose where it sets, twice it set where it rises. Yet the predicament of Egypt was in no way felt; no change appeared in the fertility of the soil nor in the favors of the Nile, the turn of sicknesses or the ravages of death.'

If they lack chonological precision or the perspective of historical reality, the priestly awareness of this long past was nevertheless not negligible; the priests knew – or could find out – a quantity of traditions related to the welfare of the kings and of the monuments of their country. The works of the Greek voyagers abound with these stories, linked with the great names of history, Sesostris, Moeris, Rhampsinite, Nitocris. . . . However, their curiosity remained alert to events outside Egypt: the Trojan war was not unknown to them, if one can believe Herodotus, and we have seen that they note in their archives the passage of scholars and Greek philosophers who came to visit their temples.

Knowing the hieroglyphic writings, they could, as we do now, learn their history in reading the monumental inscriptions with which their country was covered, although they might end by not always placing the historical episodes accurately. . . . Let us think of this old Theban priest conducting Germanicus and his escort through the ruins of the antique capital: [Tacitus, Annals II, 60].

> On these colossal constructions the Egyptian characters still existed, retracing in its entirety its ancient splendor. Asked to translate the language of his fathers, one of the old priests explained to Germanicus that the town once had 700,000 inhabitants of a military age, and with his army, the king Rameses first became master of Libya, Ethiopia, of the Medes, the Persians, the Bactrians, of Scythia and all the lands occupied by the Syrians, the Armenians, and the Cappadocians their neighbors, after which he put under his laws all that extended from the sea of Bithynia to that of Lycia. They read also the tributes imposed on the nations, the weights of silver and gold, the number of arms and horses, the offerings for the temples, ivory and perfumes, the quantities of wheat and the provisions that each nation had to furnish, tributes no less magnificent than those today imposed by the power of the Parthians or that of Rome.

As to the story of Atlantide, which a priest of Sais reported to Solon, it is easy enough to discover here some authentically Egyptian elements, which invite one to speculate on its possible origins. No doubt it is plausible to conclude, as Spanuth recently proposed, that the story of Atlantide is an Egyptian reinterpretation of ancient historical facts: one recalls in fact the gigantic invasion of the people come from the Islands in the

143

middle of the Sea, who rolled in over Libya and Egypt in the thirteenth or twelfth century before Christ and the troubles that Merenptah, then Rameses II, had in pushing them out of the Nile Valley. Entire walls, in the temple of Medinet Habu, are covered with reliefs retracing the episodes of this great battle with official poems celebrating across the country the triumph of Rameses, so that a thousand years later, the memory of it was not yet lost, and one finds the mention of these ancient hordes in the temple of Edfu. In these circumstances what is astonishing in seeing a priest of Sais cite one of the versions of this famous event? Furthermore, is not the theme of the island engulfed by the waves known, since the Middle Kingdom, through the Egyptian story of the *Naufrage*? Like the informer of Germanicus, the priest of Sais also did the work of the historian in reviving one of the glorious episodes of the past of his country, read perhaps on some temple wall, or discovered in some ancient papyrus. . . .

In conclusion, it must be recognized that history is not a science that the priests would be inclined to cultivate. Nothing in the responsibilities of their cult called for a precise knowledge of past events. But, if they did not do any intensive research in this area, nevertheless, through their knowledge of the hieratical and hieroglyphical scriptures, through their use of the old texts, through the sight of the royal tablets partially engraved in their temples for the needs of the cult, and through their habit of noting, year by year, all that happened in a day to allow them to understand omens better, or to determine their knowledge of natural phenomena, they were more able than anyone in Egypt to recount the life of their distant past.

GEOGRAPHY

Geography, however, enjoyed a certain favor among them; did not the hierogrammat have to know 'cosmography and geography. . . the topography of Egypt and the description of the Nile'? And this was not a discipline reserved to the priestly circles: we possess documents which show us the great importance which the scribes and the administration attached to the practical knowledge of their country: maps (such as that from the mining district of the Wady Fawakhir, between the Nile and the Red Sea, or that, unfortunately very dilapidated, from the district of Gebelein), lists of towns, enumerated from south to north ('onomastical'), inventories of sacerdotal property (papyrus Harris) or land surveys (papyrus Wilbour), already witness to good information. We know further that the levels of the flood were noted at various fixed points: 'when the waters of the Nile mounted to fourteen cubits, the flood was considered to have reached its maximum, and they believed they could count on the most abundant harvest; when the waters, on the other hand, only reached eight cubets, there was invariably poverty.' [Strabo] Also the 'nilometers,' placed in various defined points of the river, noted, at set dates, the height of the waters: the quai of the temple of Karnak is covered with these inscriptions showing up to what point the highest level

Map of gold mines

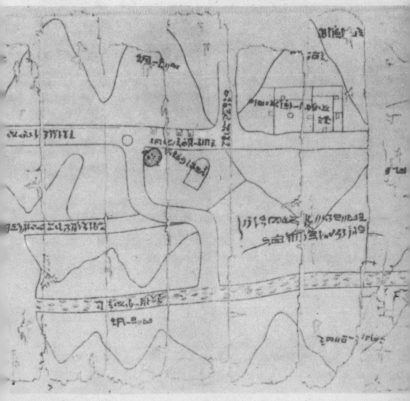

of the flood rose in such a year of such a king. The distances and the surfaces were sometimes evaluated, nome by nome, and the totals were added: the white chapel of Sesostris (temple of Karnak) contains a list of measures of this kind. . . .

Alongside this practical geography, which the priests were far from disdaining – is it not precisely on the religious edifices that the levels of the Nile as well as the measurements of the country are recorded? – existed nevertheless a religious geography of Egypt, to which the priestly circles accorded more importance: to know the towns, the distances, the surfaces of the good black earth promising harvests, was good; but to know the division of the gods in the country, the location of holy places and the centers of pilgrimages, the placement of the relics of Osiris, was better. We have thus recovered the lists of holy places – that of the cults of Osiris, for example [papyrus from the Louvre no. 3079], that of comparable goddesses, such as the litanies of Wuaset reveal to us, the compilations of all the cults of Hathor across the country [temple of Edfu], that of the relics of Osiris, whose decimated body lies in many a section of the country. . . .

It is known that, if the gods of Egypt were many, the greater part of them had no pretensions to universality; thus it was justifiable to draw, on the patterned bases of the temple walls, processions of offering bearers coming from every district of the country to give homage to the god and to bring him the tribute of their products. . . . In the Ancient Kingdom, the mastabas of the nobles are already covered with such processions; the market towns were founded in order to provide the royal funerary cult which brought in their products. Sometimes, in the temples of subsequent periods, processions can be found in which Niles (androgynous individuals) and prairies (women) alternate, loaded with the products of the fields. But very soon the idea occurred of symbolically drawing *all Egypt* carrying its tribute; each department, administrative or religious – each 'nome' – is thus represented by a Nile, carrying on his head the insignia bearing its name. But the products varied. According to its location, each city specialized in a set industry: some lived only from the fields; others prospered through outside commerce, when they were near the frontiers or the beginning of a trade route; others drew profit from mining exploitations. The tribute that the 'Nile' carries can thus vary according to the nome involved and furnishes us with precious information.

146

But in the majority of cases, these sketches are strictly religious and mention only the names, geographical or divine, which are found in connection with the theological metropolis of each *nome*. Thus these catalogues become veritable monographs of religious geography. The most famous of these lists, which is written on the sanctuary of the temple of Edfu, furnishes us, for example, the following information pertaining to each *nome:*

Name of the *nome*, name of its capital, list of its relics;
God and Goddess worshiped, and their place of cult;
Name of official priest and musician priestess;
Name of the sacred ship and of the canal on which it sails;
Name of the sacred tree growing on the holy place;
Date of principal feasts;
Religious commandments (to do this or that, to eat such and such a thing);
Name of the part of the Nile crossing the *nome*, and drawn like a winding serpent;
Name of the agricultural territory (cultivable country);
Name of the *pehou* (marshy backlands).

This inventory, repeated for each of the forty-two *nomes* of Egypt, confirmed by parallel lists of farm districts and swamps, gives a sufficient knowledge of the religious geography of the country as the priests conceived it.

But these lists, as detailed, as systematic as they may seem to us, were nevertheless only resumes of compilations otherwise more exhaustive on the subject of which we are unfortunately very poorly informed. Various indications lead us to conclude that, at least in each nome, a papyrus existed with a very detailed inventory of all the places of cult, temples, and place-names, and all the sacred objects of these edifices, of the mythological legends which were connected with each area of the district, of the feasts, and of the various soil resources. A document of this order has come down to us called the *papyrus Jumilhac,* of the Louvre Museum, revealing in all its details the religious geography and the legends of the eighteenth *nome* of Upper Egypt. The lists of sacred names inscribed in one of the crypts of the temple of Dendereh are no doubt extracts from a similar manual consecrated to the tentyrite *nome*. A fragment of lapidary inscription, found in Lower Egypt, bears several elements of an inventory of resources of the third *nome* of the Delta. One of the papyri of Tanis presents similarly annotated geographical lists. The sanctuary of the temple of Hibis preserves an actual compilation of the divinities of the countries classed by geographical sections. Everything leads us to believe that the *stela of the famine,* from which we cited above several passages, gives extracts from the book dedicated to the religious geography of the Elephantine *nome.* Let us recall the facts:

Seeking a remedy to the famine which has been raging for seven years, the king sends a priest to consult the archives of Hermopolis; on his return, the priest gave him a detailed account of all that he could find out in the region of the cataract: the following points were brought out: description of the Elephantine and enumeration of its mythological names – the Nile and the flood – the god Khnum, his epithets, his attributes – the neighboring region: mountains open for quarrying – list of the gods found in the temple of Khnum – name of the rocks that are found in the region.

Everything happens as if the priest messenger had found, in the library of Hermopolis, a complete monograph dedicated to the first *nome* of Upper Egypt, and had rapidly noted several extracts from it. Thus one may suppose that not only did each *nome* possess a detailed inventory of its mythological geography and its various resources, but that a quantity of all these monographs were found together in the library of Hermopolis, most famous of them all. It is from such archives that the 'geographical' lists which decorate the walls of the great sanctuaries were worked out.

The knowledge that the priests could have had of foreign countries was certainly less detailed – and less exact. The priestly texts often make use of names of traditional peoples, designating for example under the name 'Nine Arches' the known zones of the Egyptian world, without troubling themselves whether the peoples in question still existed under the name they used and the place they designated, as they had in the ancient times when these lists were drawn up. . . . Thus we find mentioned, at Edfu, in the first century before our era, some groups who lived under Rameses III, a thousand years earlier! Imagine a priest of the twentieth century asking the faithful to be on guard against the Huns, the Vandals, or the

Visigoths! Along with such inconsistencies of excessive tradi-
tionalism, the priestly circles had at their command appreciable
knowledge of their geographical neighbors: the lists of countries
and towns defeated by Amenophis III, Rameses II, Chechonq
I, as many in Asia as in Nubia, covered entire walls of the great
temples of Karnak and Luxor; they are obligingly displayed on
the pedestals of the royal collosi which decorate the porticos.
Let us not forget that it is probably a similar list that the old
Theban guide translated to Germanicus.

Parallel to the processions of nomes, which converge from the extremities of the temple toward the entrance of the sanctuary, lists of mining districts enumerate the African and Asian countries from which the rocks and precious metals came destined for the treasury of the god: the temples of Edfu and of Dendereh, in particular, have preserved interesting lists of this kind.

The texts of execration, of which we possess a certain number, produce perhaps some useful supplements to our information. We know that the Egyptians inscribed on the vases or statuettes of prisoners the names of Asiatic sheiks or Nubian princes that they considered dangerous to their country. These vases and statuettes were then broken or submitted to certain enchantments which were supposed to work on the enemies named, to destroy them or at least drive them out of Egypt. However these lists, dating to the Middle Kingdom, give witness to a very detailed knowledge of Asiatic and Nubian names and geography. So far, the little figures of enchantment have not been found in the temples, but we know by the texts and the reliefs that the priests kept statuettes of this kind in their sacred buildings, and they performed rites of enchantment over them: does

Magic figurine

151

not a relief in the library at Edfu show us a priest holding a whole string of these figurines strung on a cane? If it is not proven that the statuettes we possess had been produced in the temples, we know at least that the priests made use of identical figurines; it is not impossible then that the geographical knowledge to which the texts of enchantment attest was divided up, in various ways, by the priestly groups.

ASTRONOMY

If we have been able to summon up an exact enough picture of the historical and geographical knowledge of the Egyptian priestly groups, it will be infinitely more difficult to determine the extent of their information in the areas of astronomy and geometry. These two 'exact' disciplines are somewhat outside the framework of the 'humanities,' and can only be treated easily by the specialists – the Egyptologist receives their verdict with respect and recognition. The unfortunate part is that the specialists are not always of the same opinion, and it is rash to take sides. Such ineptitudes have been – and still are – written on Egyptian astronomical science and the geometrical knowledge of the priests, by the 'vulgarizers' assured of a complacent public, that scholars, with a reaction easy to understand, consent to approach the two sciences only with the greatest circumspection.

In fact, everything indicates that the Egyptians had arrived at some remarkable results in certain areas of astronomy: do we not still use, almost in detail, the calendar that they established, and have we not adopted their division of the year into twelve months and of the day into twenty-four hours? The admiring unanimity of the Greek voyagers and the appreciable number of astronomical documents found in Egypt confirm at least the interest expressed by the Ancients in celestial problems and the extent of the research they dedicated to them. What can we say in summary of their astronomical knowledge and what value must be accorded the results at which they arrived?

To believe Clement of Alexandria, the priest timekeeper had to know four scholarly works related to the order of the fixed stars, to the movements of the moon and the five planets, to the meetings and illuminations of the sun and the moon, and to the rising of the stars; on his part, the *ptérophore* had to have assimilated the second of these four treatises. These indications are in part confirmed by the Egyptian lists of priestly works, which include the knowledge of the periodical return

152

of the sun and the moon, and of the periodical return of the stars.

The Egyptians distinguished in the sky, beyond the sun and the moon, the stars which never rest – our planets: Mercury, Venus (the star of the evening and the morning), Mars (the red Horus), Jupiter (the glittering star), and Saturn (Horus the bull). They grouped the stars into constellations (different from ours, similar to the Babylonians), which it is difficult to identify. One can nevertheless recognize the Great Bear (the leg of beef), the Swan (the man with extended arms), Orion (running man looking over his shoulder), Cassiopeia (person with arms ex-

Zodiac of Athribis

tended), the Dragon and perhaps the Pleiades, the Scorpion and the Ram. The star Sirius, which they called Sothis, played a great role in their chronological calculations, its 'heliacal' rising determining the *actual* year (and delaying by one day every four years on the year of the calendar which had only 365 days). These constellations were drawn, in the form which was characteristic of them, on the ceilings of the tombs – where they replaced the habitual and more banal star-studded vault – and on the 'zodiacs' which they adopted from the Greeks, in the last epochs of their civilization. The temple of Dendereh, for example, contains one of these synthetic images of the sky, in which the constellations of the Egyptian firmament mingle, under their traditional form, the planets, the signs – imported and adapted in Nilotic style – of the twelve zodiacal figures, and the thirty-six decans.

These decans, opposite the signs of the zodiac, come from Greece, were known in Egypt from time immemorial; the zone of the sky neighboring the ecliptic had been divided by them into thirty-six sections, each one of which was watched over by a genie, each of these genies reigning on ten days of the Egyptian year. Every ten days the heliacal rising of a new decan occurred, so that the knowledge of their order, like the survey from the moment of their appearance in the course of the night, had allowed the elaboration of timetables for the rising of stars; thanks to these tables, each valid for a period of fifteen days, an observer seated on the terrace of a temple could determine the hours of the night through the successive passage in the axis of his plan of such and such star. Certain representations on the royal tombs leave one to suppose that this observation was made by means of two men, placed on a north-south axis; one, crouched and immobile as a statue, served as a landmark for the astronomer who noted the passage of the stars in the proximity of his colleague. Thus, on the sixteenth of the month of Athyr, the hours are determined as follows:

> When the star sâr was above the right eye (of the man-marker), it was 5 o'clock.
> When the arm of Orion was above the middle it was 6 o'clock.
> When the star Orion was above the left eye, it was 7 o'clock.
> When the star which follows Sothis was above the left eye, it was 8 o'clock, etc. . . .

That such a technique of determining the hour was not

154

without serious imprecision, one can easily imagine. But it was not possible to have recourse to any mechanical device: the difficulty came from the fact that the hour was not, for the Egyptians, the twenty-fourth part of the astronomical day, but the twelfth part of the *actual* duration of the day and of that of the night. In other words, day by day, the length of the hour varied, and it varied still more according to the latitude. Thus sun dials and water clocks (clepsydras) allowed them diverse systems of time reading according to the time of year. Elsewhere tables have been discovered on which the lengths of the day and the night at different times of the year were noted. One of these was used in the temple of Tanis. Insofar as it has been possible to verify its data, it permitted gross enough errors.

For the priests, the knowledge of the sky and of its mechanism served essentially, in a practical fashion, to determine the hour of the ceremonies which divided in a rigorous way the various episodes of the cult. In a less daily manner, it played an im-

Clepsydre

portant role in the determination of the cardinal points by which the religious edifices were laid out: the position of the temple was determined by celestial observations. Furthermore, the encounters of the sun and the moon (eclipses) were known to them. Have we not been told that at the time of the eclipse which terrorized the soldiers of Alexandria fighting the Persians of Darius, to calm the panic which was overcoming the troops they used the interpretation of an Egyptian priest? [Curtius Rufus, History of Alex. IV, 10.]

And we know, through a limited number of documents, that astrology, the belief in the influence of the position of the stars on individual destinies, had, in the very low epochs, some favor among the Egyptians. Everything indicates nevertheless that this belief, foreign to the Egyptian spirit, was a foreign importation. The exceptional character of the documents of this nature in the Egyptian language is proof of this.

As to the comets, whose appearance has in all times been considered a disastrous omen, they do not seem to have been well known to the ancient Egyptians [Seneca, Natural Questions II, 2]: at the most a text of Tuthmosis III speaks of the passage of one which could be Halley's comet.

GEOMETRY AND ARCHITECTURE

Perhaps it is even more difficult to describe exactly the state of priestly knowledge relating to geometry. The classic tradition is not lacking in praise of the skill of the geometer priests, and the quality of their information. But we have not found up to now any manual, any Egyptian document of any sort, that expounds the elements of geometry as they conceived it. The several papyri called 'mathematical' which have come down to us are more collections of *recipes* for solving such and such problem of arithmetic or simple geometry than manuals attesting to the knowledge of *rules* of solution: in the midst of all the problems of which they treat, empiricism and approximation are the rule. Everything leads us to believe that the knowledge of calculus and geometry, to judge from these documents, was limited to rather imperfect techniques of evaluation, limited to the practical problems before which a scribe or an architect found himself. Theoretical geometry seems absent from their preoccupations.

Thus in a celebrated literary controversy, a scribe posed the following three problems as 'sticklers' for his own colleague:

'How many bricks does it take to construct a ramp of certain dimensions?'

'How many men does it take to carry an obelisk of certain dimensions?'

'How many men does it take to empty a granary of sand in a given time?'

All this involves only relatively simple calculations, or follows from empirical inquiries estimated in the course of previous works: the moving of obelisks were usual in the New Kingdom, and the work squads had all the time necessary to be formed in a rational fashion: the heaviest statues and blocks of stone had always been moved by men, and the scribes must have had practical manuals determining the degree of handwork required in terms of the dimensions and the weight of the object to be moved.

Such is the rather misleading reply of the literary sources to our inquiry. If we now turn our eyes to the monuments, what is our impression? Constructions such as the pyramids, or the temples of Upper Egypt, bring forth such a feeling of harmony that it seems probable that these architectural figures correspond to certain blueprints of carefully described dimensions. But these blueprints, when one can find them, are basically simple, and nothing, a priori, indicates that they correspond to a secret method of expression, as is sometimes asserted. The knowledge of the priests had to include, according to the library of Edfu, a treatise on the decoration of walls. If one judges from the plan of the temples discovered and the character of their decoration, this treatise did not impose a rigorous or invariable system: there are no two temples exactly identical; no two series of scenes correspond without variation from one wall to the other. On the other hand, the general principle of the layout of the rooms and decoration presents consistent characteristics. It is probably the rules of general order of this sort which constituted the subject of this document. Perhaps one might even consider that it was a question of particular layouts relating to this same temple, with the name of its rooms, its dimensions, the particular principles of its lay out, the detail of its reliefs. A text of Petosiris leads one to suppose this [inscr. 6, 33-34; cf. 81, 70-82]. Observing in the course of a procession that the temple of Heqet was in ruins, affected a little more each year by the flood, and that its sanctuary resembled a marsh in an open field, he reclaims the sacred

book of the temple from the scribe attached to this edifice and sees on examination that the destruction was such that the foundations no longer corresponded to the book called [book of the] temple of Heqet. In each temple would thus be found a detailed plan of the construction and the decoration, explained in one or two papyri. Unfortunately we have found nothing up to now which could correspond to these documents.

As to the relative proportions of the component parts, they are far from being fixed. One can, on the reconstructions of the facades, or on the plans of the sacred buildings, find a certain number of regulating outlines: the proportions are in general very simple, and above all do not correspond to a system. Certain ratios have even been found between the height and the diameter of the columns, varying according to the style to which they are related. These are the facts which evoked more of a technical tradition of construction than the desire to inscribe subtle proportions of measures in the temple plan.

Is this to say that all geometrical expression was excluded from these constructions, and that the study of religious monuments might never reveal anything but an approximate accumulation of blocks? By no means. Even though the instruments at the architects' disposal were elementary (plumbline, square rule), the quality of the construction is nevertheless remarkable. Thus the architects obtained a perfect horizontal, at the base

158

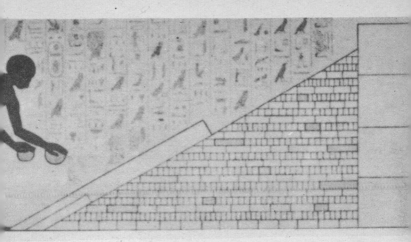

of their monuments, by digging their foundation trench up to the level of water infiltration – or by creating an artificial level in a pit lined with clay – and they carried over as a continued feature on the wall the horizontal plane that the liquid surface provided them. From this first draft they could then obtain from a series of absolutely horizontal layers a height that could reach the walls: to do this, technical ability and care evidently took the place of precision instruments which they did not seem to have known.

We know further that orientation played a great role in the plans of their religious edifices, as every foundation begins in a stellar design and the plans of axes, often multiple, have been on various occasions drawn up on the foundation slabs of different rooms. To what did they correspond? What rules define their orientation? It is premature to decide this. A recent work treating of astronomical orientation regrets, for the great mass of monuments, the imprecision of the extracts on which one must work, and underlines the hazardous character of the conclusions that one could draw from insufficient models. Few edifices were erected with such care that the reading of their plans could be as eloquent as the examination of the original itself. Aside from several great collections, the Theban group (Medinet Habu, Luxor, Karnak, Esna) and a few others, to which the architects brought a special effort, one must unfortunately recognize that the vast majority of Egyptian monuments were erected in too premature or schematic fashion, for one to decide, in the parallel examination of their architectural characteristics, if there were fixed rules determining their orientation and the placement of their axes, or if, outside an explanation valid for all, each case resulted from particular local conditions.

In conclusion then, here is what stands out in the Egyptian sources: the geometrical knowledge of the Egyptians seems to have been rather summary, to judge by the 'mathematical' texts which they have left us. However, several religious monuments,

Foundation ritual (Temple of Edfu)

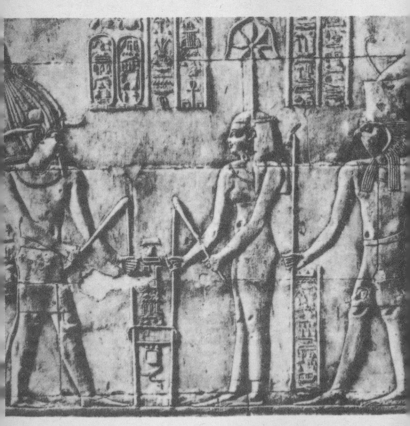

studied with particular care, have revealed an astonishing technical perfection – united with the desire to express, through the geometrical proportions of architectural masses and of elements of construction, a certain harmony of simple proportions. The possibility of more complex tendencies seems to emerge from a few recent statements, but still too few in number for the results obtained to be able to give rules having a general application.

MEDICINE

Neither the lists of priestly books nor the inventory of the sacred wisdom which Clement of Alexandria has passed on to us make mention of medical works. It seems at first glance, in fact, that such a science was foreign to the preoccupations of the cults and that the religious service had no need of its practice. Nevertheless we know that medicine was practiced in the Houses of Life; a relief from the temple of Kom Ombo shows a collection of 'surgical instruments' and several medical texts have been found in the vast lot of papyri from the temple of Tebtunis; furthermore, some of the priests' titles show us their competence in certain areas of medicine. Specialized texts, such as the *Edwin Smith Surgical Papyrus,* testify to very rational knowledge and practices, but general belief – still widespread in our day among the fellahs of Upper Egypt – would have it that sicknesses were sent by the terrible goddess Sekhmet, when they did not arise simply from the malevolence of some perverse spirit, from the evil eye cast by an enemy, or from the hostility of some ghost. . . . It was less a question, in popular opinion, of fighting the physical cause of illness than of exorcising the evil demon and forcing him to let go of his prey. Nothing, to assure such a result, like a good magic formula – and nobody so qualified to administer it as some scholarly 'priest-reader,' versed in the knowledge of the old magic books, and able to mix, in an irresistible formula, all the resources of the old magic. Thus our learned masters of ritual often acted outside the temple as village sorcerers. . . .

Other priests were more specialized. If Sekhmet, the formidable lioness, could cause sickness, she could also cure it. Her priest, the superior of priests of Sekhmet, is renowned for his medical knowledge, specializing however in animal illnesses; one would consider him rather a veterinary. . . . Similarly the priest of Selqit, the scorpion-goddess, was particularly apt in

161

curing illness resulting from venomous bites. It is probable that the personnel of certain god-healers, such as Imhotep, who became, in the low epoch and in the Greek tradition, Imouthes, son of Ptah, had highly developed medical knowledge, or at least were considered especially qualified to cure illnesses. Thus we know that the medical competence attributed by the popular piety of the low epochs to Amenophis, son of Hapou, the architect of king Amenophis III, was exploited by his clergy in a commercial fashion. His cult moved out of his funerary temple – in ruins already in this epoch – to a superior chapel of the temple of Deir el Bahari, more fit to receive the faithful. And the renown of the cures and miracles that he accomplished brought the crippled of the entire world to his chapel. They wrote on its walls the story of their cure or mention of their visit. . . . Other sanatoria of this kind existed in Egypt, for example at Abydos. But nothing enables us to decide if faith alone – encouraged by a scholarly propaganda – performed the miracles, or if the clergy of these gods were endowed with medical knowledge likely to sustain, by their effectiveness, the renown of their patron. At least we can note that the Greek tradition reports that Hippocratus, then later Galen, were inspired in their medical researches by the books kept in the library of the temple of Imhotep at Memphis.

ANIMAL SCIENCE

According to Clement of Alexandria, the stolist had to know the science of animal markings. We learn from Herodotus of what this science consists. For an animal to be sacrificed, it was first necessary for a qualified priest to pronounce it *pure*. And here is how this examination went:

> If one ascertains on the body of an ox the presence of a single black hair, one considers the animal impure. The inspector is a priest committed to this concern; he examines the beast standing and lying on its flank, pulls out its tongue to see if it is contaminated with any conspicuous blemish. . . ; he sees also if the hairs of the tail are arranged in normal fashion. If the animal has no blemish, he marks it by rolling around its hooves a papyrus; he applies clay and puts his seal on it; they then lead the beast away. To sacrifice an ox which is not marked is to risk death.

It is likely that each of the animals which could be sacrificed

– and they were numerous, from birds and fish to antelope and oxen – had to fulfill certain conditions of purity. No doubt the stolist had to know as well the forbidden animals, and their distribution in the religious geography of the country: they were numerous, as one can judge by the list we have cited.

But his competence had to excel in an activity that was especially important to the religious life of the temples: the designation of the sacred animal. Sometimes, as is the case at Edfu and at Philae, an animal – here a falcon – was chosen each year to incarnate the divinity for twelve months. In other places, at Memphis for example, the animal was chosen and enthroned until his death: this is the case of the bull Apis. When an Apis died and rejoined, in the vast subterranean lands of Serapeum, at Saqqara, the mummies of his predecessors, a great quest commenced throughout the country until one was found to replace him. There were numerous prerequisites:

> He must be born of a cow who could not conceive again. The Egyptians claim that a flash of lightning fell from the sky on this cow, and that from this lightning she conceived the bull Apis. This young bull called Apis could be recognized by the following

Votive group (Louvre Museum)

signs: black, he bears on his brow a white triangle, on his back the figure of an eagle; the hairs of his tail are double; under his tongue is the figure of a scarab. [Herodotus III, 28.]

It is probable that this science of markings revealing the sacred character of an animal extended to the complete list of divine beasts: from Apis, the ram of Mendes, the bull Boukhis, the crocodile of the Fayoum, to innumerable varieties of animals

which here or there could be, in some manner, considered as marked by divine selection. . . . [cf. Greek papyrus of Lund.]

THE INTERPRETATION OF DREAMS

The Greek lists enumerating the various members of the priestly colleges make mention of the *oneirocrites*, 'the interpreter of dreams.' We know in fact that the faithful had the custom, in the low epoch, of sleeping in the temple, in the hope of a premonitory dream which could indicate to them what they had to do – or even reveal to them a part of the future. This is what the magician Horus, son of Panishi, did, in the demotic story to which we have already made numerous references, when he could not discover a way of saving the Pharaoh from the sorceries of the Ethiopians.

When the dream was not a direct prediction of the future, when it was necessary to interpret in a certain way the nocturnal visions – mysterious from the beginning – they would turn to a specialist. We recall the story of Joseph explaining to the Pharaoh the significance of the seven fat years and the seven lean years. . . . In the papyrus of the Theban necropolis, collections of dream interpretations were found in which the facts are classified as follows: a general title: if a man sees himself in his dream. . .; then two parallel columns: to the left: doing such and such thing; to the right: it is good (or: it is bad); this means that. . . . Here are some sample extracts from this manual:

If a man sees himself in his dream
drinking wine – good – [it is] that he will open his mouth to speak;
sitting in a tree – good – [it is] the destruction of all his woes;
killing a goose – good – [it is] to kill his enemies;
visiting Bousiris – good – [it is] to reach a great age;
looking into a great pit – bad – [it is] his placement in prison;
catching fire – bad – he will be massacred;
seeing a dwarf – bad – half of his life will be severed . . . etc.

This collection is from the New Kingdom; from the low epoch, we possess a series of similar interpretations which show that the technique was far from being lost: the processes, like the nature of dreams, remained perceptibly identical.

This 'science' was reserved to the members of the clergy. Is it not characteristic to see that, in the coptic translation of Genesis (XLI, 8 and 24), the name designating the magicians who were called to interpret the dream of the Pharaoh was precisely that of 'Scribes of the House of Life'?

We cannot, without some abuse, rank magic among the priestly *sciences*. In the eyes of the priests, however, the knowledge of adequate formulas furnished a nearly unlimited power over living beings, the gods, and the forces of the universe. The magician was a dangerous being who could not be held back for an instant by the most spectacular exploits: 'I will beat the earth into the depths of the water, the South will become the North, and the earth will be overturned. . . .' In practice, however, we hope their ambitions were more modest. The effect that they expected from magical practice was nevertheless perfectly worthy: the magnificent order that the gods had established on earth was perpetually threatened by the revolt of perverse forces, bad spirits, adulterated souls of the dead, obscure and malevolent powers. But in the inmost part of the temple there was a little of the divine substance infused in the images, in each of the figures of the gods graven the length of the walls. This divine presence lessened progressively, dissolved, lost its intensity to the point that, each year, the images had to be 'recharged' with their divine potential. . . . The approach of obscure powers directly threatened the god living in the temple: thus the magical practices of enchantment had as their end to chase out the demons from the temple: the lists enumerate for us the books for capturing enemies, for protecting the king in his palace – and he needed it. Remember the Ethiopian sorceries which beat him while he slept! To repel the evil eye. . . . In the course of excavations, quantities of sacerdotal works of this kind have been found: books on overthrowing Apopi, the enemy of Re and Osiris, ritual for beating Seth and his associates, ritual for repulsing the angry; the well-known rites of hunting with a snare and those of the breaking of the red vases, putting the magic force in the service of the king and the State.

Such was the official aspect of the magic practices. But the gods were not the only ones to benefit: the priest-reader was grand master in sorcery and in his civilian life made a profession of exorcism; he made out prescriptions against fever, against scorpion bites, against illnesses of all sorts. On occasion, he worked out some love charm, destined to break the last scruples of a too reticent beauty – without always sacrificing the conditions to gallantry: 'make her follow me, as a bull follows its fodder, as a servant follows his children, as a shepherd follows his flock. . . .' As to the beauty, she had an amulet whose role

166

was at least as devoid of ambiguity: 'rise and bind the one with whom I am concerned to make him my lover!...'

The field of magic and the number of its procedures were practically unlimited. Let us recall simply two rather strange areas in which the priests of Egypt passed as masters. The first will hardly astonish those who know the climate of Egypt and the immutable blue of its sky: this was the art of making rain. Several documents attest to the belief that the magicians could, by their incantations, make a storm gather, and an episode in the wars of Marcus Aurelius, in the course of which the Roman army was saved from disaster thanks to miraculous rain unleashed by Harnouphis, 'hierogrammat of Egypt,' comes, in an unexpected way, to confirm this tradition. The second is a process of divination by means of a vase filled with water covered with a thin film of oil, before which a child kneels, serving as medium. The magician commands the child to open his eyes: if he sees light in the mirror of oil, contact is established with the gods: the future can then reveal its secrets, one by one.

DRUGS AND PHARMACY

Although they indicate a technique very special in itself,

Statue of a healer (Louvre Museum)

we can attribute to the priestly bodies of knowledge the formulas for drugs. The library of Edfu in fact makes mention of a book knowing all the secrets of the laboratory – that is to say the recipes for the production of the salves and heady perfumes which delighted the gods. The temples sometimes included little offices which served as storehouses for odoriferous products. [Karnak: XVIII dynasty; Esna: Roman epoch.] In the temple of Edfu, a room of stone, designated by the name of 'laboratory,' had its walls covered with hieroglyphic recipes revealing the technique for preparing various liturgical perfumes, the basic elements, the amount to mix, the time for cooking or freezing, etc. . . . One of these recipes, particularly detailed, tells how to make a half litre of superfine extract of storax.

The following ingredients must be procured:

Essence of carob-bean	575 cm³
Dry incense of first quality	1.010 gr.
Rind of storax of first quality	600 gr.
Aromatic calame	25 gr.
Asphalt (wood of convolvulus scoparius L)	10 gr.
Mastic (resin of pistacia lentiscus L)	10 gr.
Grain of violet (?)	15 gr.
Very alcoholic wine	0 l. 500 cm³
Water	

. From these products, eight successive operations, spread over eight days, allowed one to obtain after innumerable mixings, cookings, decantations, a small quantity of cosmetic. It therefore took much care – much patience as well – to prepare these subtle perfumes which were then scattered over the statues in the course of the ceremonies of the cult. But unfortunately we are not always able to know if the result justified the months of work required.

LITERATURE

From history to pharmacy, geography, astronomy, geometry, medicine, and magic, the areas of priestly wisdom are revealed as exceptionally vast and varied. Certain of these sciences – of these techniques – are the domain of specialists. Each priest – and we have seen the multiplicity of functions and skills which could be covered by this too general name – possessed some elements of this wisdom, attached to the role that he had to carry out in the divine cult. There were few men, certainly, who could flatter themselves that they possessed all of it. Although this idea of the *specialization* of knowledge is indisputable, the various members of the clergy were related to each other by something profound. Beyond these practical specializations which differentiated them, there was a general religious and intellectual culture in which all the participants in the cult – at least among the high clergy – equally participated. Born of common preoccupations, of meditation on the same philosophical and religious problems, of readings from the same old texts, composed somewhat of a synthesis of all the disciplines that we have examined; sustained finally by the awareness the priests had of belonging to a group privileged to guard and interpret tradition, this priestly culture was no doubt as remarkable as it was general. At least it sustained, among those who benefited from it, a constant intellectual curiosity. It appears to us, from this point of view, rather characteristic that literary preoccupations were not foreign to the sacred personnel of the temples. No doubt the libraries of the sanctuaries possessed no profane works – a worker does not carry a novel to the factory! But outside the hours of religious service, the priests took pleasure in romances which were popular at the time. Thus the archives of Tebtunis have revealed examples on papyrus of the great action of Petoubastis, like the story of Satni. On occasion, the scribes of the House of Life, literate by profession, wrote original works: thus we have become acquainted recently with the beginning of a text of instruction from the New Kingdom, which was the work of a clerk named Amennakhte. The fragments of literature [Insinger Papyrus] found at Tebtunis show that the production of similar writings, common among the lay scribes, was in no way disdained among the priestly circles. Had we doubted this, the texts of Petosiris and the addresses to the clergy of Edfu, from which we have cited extracts above, would have sufficed to enlighten us.

There were periods when sacerdotal wisdom was – except in a few rare areas – only a reflection of the general knowledge of the technicians, scribes, wise men of Egyptian society. It even happened that some particularly important scientific documents – and even some 'lay' theological texts – came from spheres absolutely foreign to the temples.

With time we nevertheless witness a certain concentration of the Egyptian scientific heritage in the priestly circles: the profound modification, with the Greek occupation, of the living conditions of the administrative services, whose schools were already centers of culture; the progressive retreat to the temples of all that remained of the traditional and the national in Egypt, contributed little by little to making the Egyptian priest the representative type of lettered man and scholar. Thus the opinion of the Greek voyagers is confirmed, as we have mentioned above – as well as that of the Arab authors, who echoed the same flattering tradition. To the exalted idea they jointly held of sacred wisdom, we can now add that this knowledge was not a simple juxtaposition of techniques, but corresponded, in its universality as in the philosophical and moral ideas to which it gave rise, to a genuine and appreciable culture.

Key of dreams

FORTUNES AND MISFORTUNES
OF THE EGYPTIAN CLERGY

After these several chapters of ethnography, it is time to construct a little history and to speak of the clergies. What we have said of the priesthood, of the conditions for entering it, of the religious and moral life of the priests, of their wisdom, constitutes a synthesis generally correct, but necessarily schematic: made of many elements, borrowed from all periods of history, it offers a typical picture of the priestly classes, statistically valid, but in which there is a place neither for individual details nor for modifications produced by history. It is this last perspective on the ecclesiastical world that we will attempt to open up.

Nothing was more foreign to the spirit of the Egyptians than the idea of a possible separation between Church and State. Never was religion a *private* phenomenon to which individual choice could give more or less importance: as in the distant times of the prehistoric clans, it is the same structure of social and national life, whose direction was in the hands of the sovereign. Thus the fate of the clergies and the wealth of the gods are strictly connected to political circumstances.

When, a little before the dawn of history, the clans undertook the conquest of the country, they each did so under the leadership of a chief and the protection of a god; the victory of a clan confirmed the power of its god and increased his prestige.

The political empire of the kings increased with the spiritual power of the gods. How better to reward a divinity and encourage his benevolence than by enriching his temple and multiplying the number of his servants? The royal court gained in pomp and in importance at each extension of the conquests – and therefore for the god and his earthly domain. The earth, we know, was the property of the sovereign: in giving the god a part of this land, the king assured the material life of his clergy, guaranteed the regularity of his offerings, and thereby interested the god in the political fate of his dynasty. We recall the moving episode of the 'battle of Kadesh' in which Rameses, encircled and abandoned by his own, called on his father Amon for help:

> Amon, my father, what is happening?
> Does a father thus forget his son? . . .
> Have I not raised innumerable monuments to thee,
> Have I not filled thy temple with my captives?
> It is for thee I built my temple for millions of years,
> and I have made thee a veritable gift of all my goods.
> I consecrate all foreign countries to the service of thy offerings,
> and I offer thee tens of thousands of oxen, as well as all kinds of plants with sweet perfume.
> Nothing beautiful have I omitted to make in thy sanctuary.
> I have raised for thee imposing pylons,
> and I myself erected their flagpoles.
> I had brought forth for thee obelisks from Elephantine,
> and it was also I who had the granite transported.
> I launched ships for thee on the green sea
> to bring to thee the tribute of barbarian countries.
> It would be astonishing to have misfortune happen to one bent to thy will. . . .
> On the contrary favor one who reveres thee, and he will serve thee with love!

The king enriched the god with his earthly goods, and in exchange the god helped the king in his military enterprises: the favor of the gods, their material wealth, would be tied to the political success of the kings.

On the other hand, we can imagine that the unlimited accumulation of wealth of a god could, at length, constitute a menace

172

to the royal authority. There were periods, in the New Kingdom, when the clergy of Amon was richer and more powerful than the king himself: the statistics carried by the Harris papyrus and already cited earlier are eloquent in this regard: more than 80,000 men, and more than 770 square miles of land belonged to the one clergy of the Theban god. . . . The god patronizes the sovereign, assures the triumph of his dynasty, extends his victories to the limits of the known world, but the king, in exchange, splits with the god – and especially with his increasingly voracious clergy – the fruits of his successes.

The religious history of Egypt is thus marked, in every period, by an official double attitude of the kings, apparently contradictory: considering the dynastic god as the all-powerful ally who assures his own glory, and who has the right to the most sumptuous attentions; but, at the same time, watching with a distrustful eye the scope of the clergies whose appetite and needs never ceased to grow – always beyond the favors conceded them. To enrich the god, to overwhelm with gifts, to increase the temples in his name and spread his glory, this was the effect of a legitimate filial attitude – and of a well-understood interest. But to create and maintain, in the service of this god, a clergy always more numerous, ever more powerful, a veritable state within a state, which could on occasion impose its will on the sovereign, this was assuming a risk the dangers of which were clearly perceptible. Thus, when we will have revealed, in a few paragraphs, the successive scope of the great clergies of Egypt, we will have yet to examine the efforts spent by the central power on assuring the control of these priestly encroachments, then to describe the several great crises which gave rise to this latent antagonism.[1]

What was the real history of these predynastic clans, the actual extent of their conquests, the success and geographical diffusion of their cults? It is not easy, even now, to determine this. To point on a map to all the regions of Egypt where the cult of the same divinity is found in order to see, in this distribution, the survival of prehistoric empires, constituted under the aegis of a god, then progressively divided, would be exagger-

1. The royalty and the clergy are like two vessels of an hourglass . The wealth and power pass in turn from one to another: the clergy exhausts the forces of royalty, then the latter rudely takes back what it had given. [Cf. Preaux.]

atedly simple. To reconstitute, on the other hand, the entire prehistory of the Delta and Upper Egypt creeds in transposing to historical life the antagonism of the theologies which are witnessed to, in the fifth dynasty, by the Texts of the Pyramids, remains an enterprise as brilliant as it is risky; Sethi, who took an interest in this, has constructed a whole history of Egypt before Menes on these very weak clues: at the base of his system is the idea that the Texts of the Pyramids were very ancient religious rituals, predating by a number of centuries their first printing on the funerary monuments. Their diversity corresponded to that of the political states whose ancient antagonism they express. He sees thus a first tentative grouping in the Delta, in which the two kingdoms of Osiris and Horus fuse, then launch themselves on the conquest of the South against the worshipers of Seth. To this first unified Egypt a state relying on the young Heliopolitan theology would have succeeded whose sun god Re could instantly rally all support; then, a third tentative unification, led this time by the Horian kingdoms of the South against the Delta; from then on Horian itself would have led, at the dawn of history, to the decisive conquests of the king-Scorpion and of Menes.

One can imagine all the uncertainty and caprice that this brilliant reconstruction may perhaps permit. Nothing is absolutely proved – except certain graphic and grammatical divergences. The various rituals at the base of the texts of the Pyramids pertain to different historical periods, especially transmitted, transposed in a mythological form, the echo of the state wars of the two preceding millenia. Without rejecting an attempt at historical reconstruction which recommends itself by an admirable rigor and by the satisfying succession of facts that it describes, certain scholars are more inclined, at present, to accord a shorter history to the Texts of the Pyramids; perhaps archaeology, more than the study of religious texts, will furnish the basic facts which will some day allow us to trace the history of these distant periods.

Whatever had been the fate of the prehistoric clans, certain divinities benefited, at the dawn of history, from the success of their worshipers. Thus the falcon god Horus, patron of Hieraconpolis in Upper Egypt, as of the extreme Behedet of the Delta, remained, for the entire duration of Egyptian civilization, the dynastic patron god of the king: it is through comparison with this god that the king received a name, his name

174

Stela of the serpent king (Louvre Museum)

of Horus, inscribed in the interior of the design of a palace above which the sacred bird sits enthroned.

But another divinity succeeded in winning the favor of the kings. The capital of the Ancient Kingdom was established at Memphis, some distance to the south of the point of the Delta: there had been several attempts to advance, for a brief period, gods like Seth, then Ptah, to a certain dynastic power, but these attempts were without a future. In turn the Heliopolitan religion, which revered the sun Re, did not delay in imposing its supremacy: a first attempt had taken place under Djeser (around 2800 B.C.); then, after a short interval, the idea took hold, and the kings proclaimed thereafter, almost without interruption, the sun god: the title 'son of Re' became a permanent part of their official name. A story is told of how the fourth Memphite dynasty (2720-2560 B.C.) had to cede place to the heirs born of the god Re in a town on the western border of the Delta. Beginning with Sahura (around 2500 B.C.), nearly all the kings introduced the divine name on the inside of their shields. The importance of the solar temples on the left bank of the Nile, the position of the pyramids, the documents, the texts, give witness to the prodigious scope of this solar religion, and its constant extension under the royal patronage.

OSIRIS

Another god of the Delta, known very early, Osiris, was soon spread throughout the country: his success is less due to the political destiny of his worshipers than to the funerary character of his attributes. God of the dead, he seems, from his Busiris birth, to have rapidly gained a very vast kingdom of worshipers; in some centuries, he was known in all Egypt. He became established about the eleventh dynasty (around 2050 B.C.), in the great city of Abydos, where throughout Egyptian history, he was the great sovereign of the dead, the guarantor of immortality. It seems however that the clergy of this god was contented with the eminent role that popular belief lent to Osiris and did not nourish political ambitions: perhaps it is this moderation which spared him the fate of certain other gods, who lived no longer than the kings whose accession they had patronized. . . . In the low epochs, when old Heliopolis was no more than a deserted town, and the opulent Thebes nothing but a great field of ruins, the cult of Osiris and Isis was more widespread than ever, winning over the Greek islands, Rome,

Osiris

and even the forests of Germany. . . . In Egypt itself there was
no temple, to whatever god it might be consecrated, which did

not reserve some chapel to the cult of the great god of the dead, and some rites at feast days to his resurrection.

Amon

Strangely unknown to the ancient epochs, we witness during the Middle Kingdom the rise to power of a Theban god to whom the most fruitful destiny was reserved. God of the great Amenemhat kings, then, at the time of the Hyksos occupation, god of the national resistance which finally triumphed, Amon rapidly won, between the twentieth and twenty-fifth centuries before our era, the title of 'king of the gods,' and the firm position of all-powerful protector of the Theban sovereignty. Solidly installed in the capital of Upper Egypt, enriched by the royal conquests and by the wealth that the colonialism of the Amenophis and the Tuthmosis brought to the valley, its clergy organized and developed, populating a religious city of a size never before attained, it eclipsed by its youthful power all the popularity that the old divinities of the capitals could, here and there, still enjoy. We have already described its material power, and underlined its wealth: by the oracle of its god, patron of the monarchy, it became all-powerful in the State, and royal favor was more a necessary homage conceded to its power than the expression of a filial piety freely given.

THE STRUGGLES FOR LEADERSHIP OF THE CULTS AND THE CRISES OF THE NEW KINGDOM

The sole official agent of the cults, the Pharaoh always remained the spiritual head of the religion of the temples. But the extension of the 'temporal' power of the gods and the organization of their goods required a control that he could not assure. Thus, from the time of the Ancient Kingdom, the function of 'chief of all the religious offices,' was established and conferred by the king first to members of his family, then to the vizir. It was a guardian function, which allowed the central power to exercise a superior authority over the clergy and, if the case arose, to balance their power.

The last dynasties of the Ancient Kingdom commemorate the fall of the central authority and the administrative and political division of the country. The lords of the provincial capitals – the nomarchs – crowded forward to enjoy this state of things, to take control of the cults of their department: they bore among their titles thereafter, 'chief of the prophets,' and the administration of the temples was in some way subordinated to them.

Later the title of 'chief of the prophets of the South and the

North appeared, corresponding to a veritable ministry over the cults of Egypt – a pontificate. Around this title raged a storm of greed. It went first to the vizir, who affirmed the sovereignty of the central administration and of the king over the temporal power of the gods. But soon the priests of Amon succeeded in winning it for the chief of their prophets who perpetuated the prevailing role of their god in the State – and of their clergy in the political life of the country. This conquest dates from the reign of Tuthmosis III; the priests seem to have come then to the height of their power. But we shall see that already a royal reaction was brewing which would lead the Amonian clergy very near its downfall.

THE BEGINNING OF THE SOLAR REACTION

With Tuthmosis III (1483-1450 B.C.) a theological reaction began which tends to remind one of the former popularity of the old Heliopolitan solar cult, neglected meanwhile because of the success of Amon. The start was very slow, and was not marked right away by any brutal events. We note that in the meantime the king started to reconstruct a host of temples, which the poverty of previous times had practically ruined. This already restored vigor to certain cults foreign to the Amonian theology; and the solar temples played a large part in this: the repair of the old sanctuary of Re at Sakhebu, obscure town of the Delta, is characteristic of this tendency. It continued under Amenophis II and Tuthmosis IV did everything possible to restore the cults of the Memphite region to favor, among others that of Harmakhis, the sphinx of Giza, syncretic form of the solar divinity. Under Amenophis III – sign of the times! – the function of 'chief of the prophets of the South and of the North' slipped away from the clergy of Amon, who only recovered it under Rameses II. But the rupture did not take place until some years later, under the reign of Amenophis IV.

THE AMARNIAN EPISODE

There is little chance that the heresy of Amenophis IV – Akhenaten will ever be explained in terms which fully satisfy the soul of the scholars and the curiosity of readers. The strangeness of the royal portraits, hesitating between a sickly sweetness and a demoniac expressiveness, the not very Egyptian charm of the queen Nofretete, the touching intimacy of the familial scenes that the artists enjoy depicting, the magnificent inspiration which

Akhenaten and Nofretete

enlivens the solar hymns – everything contributes to making the
Amarnian episode an astonishing niche in a world we had thought
we knew well, an historical and psychological phenomenon
whose key will long be denied us. Political reaction? Whim of
a soul of exceptional feeling and sensitive to a more personal
religion than that of the official clergy? Simple quarrel of
theologians? All theories have been put forth; all appear to
have some truth; none suffices to explain all the facts.

It remains that Amenophis IV abandoned Thebes and his king god, to found, in Middle Egypt, a new city (the present Tell el Amarna) which was dedicated solely to the god that he worshiped in his heart, Aton, the radiant disc with a thousand arms. It was not simply a question of some new aspect of faith which could be put alongside all the others: the religion of Akhenaten was *exclusive*; the temples were closed, the names of the gods proscribed, and sanctuaries of the new cult constructed in all the large cities of Egypt – even at Karnak, in the vicinity of the temples of Amon. . . .

The death of Amenophis IV sounded the knell of the religion of the disc. After a very short stay in the capital of Aton, his successor, the young Tut-ankh-amon, left Tell el Amarna, '*the horizon of the disc*,' and returned to Thebes, where he published a decree abolishing all the measures formerly taken against the gods of Egypt. After twenty years of vigilance, the clergy of Amon reemerged stronger than ever. But it was soon to find itself up against new rivals.

THE SETHIAN EPISODE

The new dynasty in power, so careful that it should appear to 'restore everything to order,' had many reasons for mistrusting the Amonian clergy. Descendants of a military family of the Eastern Delta, the new kings were traditionally devoted to a god little esteemed by the masses, because of the role that he took in the death of Osiris, but they preserved nevertheless, here and there, the centers of this cult of the god Seth. The Amarnian experience showed what it could cost to break too abruptly with the beliefs that the entire nation shared, and to enter into open warfare against a clergy as powerful, in practice, as the monarchy itself. Thus the politics of Sethi (1312-1301 B.C.) and of Rameses II (1301-1235 B.C.) were infinitely more subtle than those of their predecessors. First there was no rupture with Thebes: the constructions continued; grandiose edifices were raised to the glory of Amon, at Karnak (hypostyle hall), at Gourna, and at Ramesseum. But Rameses went to seek in the region of Abydos the sovereign pontiff of the Amonian clergy! . . . Then he gave his favors to the Memphite and Heliopolitan cults, not hesitating to install two of his sons, Merytum and Khamuast, as high priests of Re and of Ptah, and showing, by his buildings and his politics, an ever increasing confidence in the great divinities of the north; finally, wearied of Thebes and of its too enterprising priests, he went to build a new capital, Pi-Rameses, in the Eastern Delta, where he could worship at his ease the gods dearest to him, and accord to Amon only second place.

Parallel to the three gods, as they thus heaped up the most flattering attentions, Sethi and Rameses showed an obvious predilection for their familial god, Seth. But there also they moved with prudence: in Egyptian thought, Seth remained the criminal god responsible for the death of Osiris, and the soverĕigns could not think of promoting him without raising nearly unanimous protest. Thus – as a preventive measure – Sethi dedicated a good part of his activity to the maintenance and extension of the Osirian temples of Abydos, while Rameses, not content to have raised in this same city a number of edifices, promoted Nebounnef to the supreme pontificate of the clergy of Amon. After these signs of solicitude, the supporters of Osiris could hardly resent as a personal offense the favor that the kings showed the god Seth: especially as this aggrandizement of Seth – like the enrichment of the Heliopolitan and Memphite gods – did not threaten the clergy of Osiris, but rather that of Amon.

The provincial metropolises where Seth had been worshiped from all eternity, Ombos, Tjebu, Sepermeru, received some new glory from the favor accorded by the Ramesside leaders to the god of the Eastern Delta. Above all, Pi-Rameses, the new capital, brilliantly restored the worship that Seth had formerly received in the Avaris of the Hyksos.

Without breaking with Amon, Sethi and Rameses were thus able to weaken his power a little, and they had seen to it, in heaping on Osiris unequaled favors, that the god Seth could benefit in the country by a certain sympathy. This was the result of a magnificent political sense; their successors were not always so skillful.

It did not escape the partisans of Amon that the revival of Seth, the foundation of a new capital in the Delta, the favor accorded the cults of Re and Ptah, were not simple coincidences; under the apparent favors that the monarchy granted them, they perceived the uneasy sovereigns' ill-disguised distrust of the excessive power that Amon had come to acquire and to maintain, despite the serious crisis of the cult. The fears of the Theban clergy nevertheless did not last long: the dynastic favor to Seth did not extend beyond several decades, and soon a general movement began against the outcast god who tended more and more to incarnate all the evil forces hostile to the country; both on a religious and a political level, Seth was considered the murderer of Osiris, whose popularity had not ceased to grow. Seth was also the god of the invaders who during the last centuries preceding Alexander came to succeed one another on Egyptian soil. . . . Thus for a second time Amon triumphed over rival cults which the monarchy had attempted to impose.

THE KING-PRIESTS

The last Rameses kings had not been particularly energetic sovereigns. Thus the clergy of Amon, emerging triumphant from

Seth

two grave crises and having succeeded in regaining the favor of the kings had to spend little effort to overcome the final obstacle which separated it from supreme power. Accustomed from then on to choosing the kings and skilled at supporting them, the clergy had every reason to invest itself, in the person of its high priest, with the royal office. A first attempt in this direction seems to have failed: the high priest Amenophis, too ambitious, was removed by Rameses XI; royalty scored a point. But a little while later, a military man, Herihor, who took the title of first prophet of Amon, launched himself on the conquest of power, supported by the army and the Theban clergy. The king had first to consent to share his power with the new pontiff; then, progressively, the official sovereign seems to disappear; hardly any more is said of Rameses: it remains only a question of Herihor. Finally the name of the latter appears in a cartouche: the Ramesside monarchy has evacuated, replaced for a while by the clergy of Amon.

What this priestly royalty would be is easy to imagine: the equilibrium of the state required not only the alliance of religious power and the royal office, it also needed the efforts of royal *action*, organizational and conquering. But Egypt of the twenty-first dynasty lived within itself; Lebanon scorned it, and Nubia had nearly forgotten its proximity: the wealth of the colonial lands which formerly flowed in were no more than a distant memory.

Thus, for lack of personal prestige, for lack of real authority, the clergy reigned by the voice of its god: Amon gave out his decrees regarding everything; the political weakness of the priestly sovereigns hid itself behind the scarecrow of the divine oracle. . . .

With the subsequent dynasties, the clergies of the Delta regained some advantage, in particular that of the goddess Bastet. Amon, in distant Thebes, slept. The replacing of the high priest by the divine worshiper at the head of his clergy did not end by restoring any authority to him: on the contrary, the succession regulated itself from then on by adoption, and the clergy fell entirely into the hands of political power – that of the kings of the Delta, that of the conquering 'Ethiopians,' and, a little later, that of the Saite sovereigns.

THE LAST CENTURIES OF THE NATION

The kings of the new dynasty showed themselves favorable

to the temples of the Delta, those of Sais, their first capital, and all those of the cities and towns, as they became enriched through the development of a system regulated by donations of land and of immunities. They did not have great fear of these little religious towns. They were too numerous and too full of rival interests. On the other hand the Thebaide, distant and organized, constituted a more serious threat. In adopting as 'divine worshipers' the nordic princesses, and in attaching to them a high major-domo, the Saite sovereigns could hope to control in effective fashion the life of the Amonian clergy: and which marked the effective return of religious power to the Pharaoh.

Of the fate of the Egyptian clergies during the sixth, fifth, and fourth centuries, we know nothing which can enlighten us concerning their actual power and their hopes of domination. Thebes was in complete decay: the pillage of the Assyrians, in 663, then the Saite control over the cults of the country, had seriously reduced their ambitions. Other cults were developing, supported by popular favor, mainly those of Osiris and Isis, to which chapels were being constructed everywhere. Under the last Egyptian kings, the Nectanebos, a great program of reconstruction seems to have been put into action: most of the religious buildings received new doors and new enclosures; new temples were under construction – those of Philae and of Behbeit el Hagar in particular, dedicated to Isis. Egypt, little by little, took its definitive architectural aspect at the moment that the second Persian conquest and the arrival of the Macedonian Alexander (332 B.C.) came to put a finish to its status as a free nation.

THE GREEK AND ROMAN EPOCH

What became of the Egyptian clergies under the domination of the Lagides? We have already emphasized the strangeness of the *trade* that had passed implicitly between the sovereign and the priests: the latter, still very powerful, could effectively serve the central power by keeping up before the people the fiction of its legitimacy; but the king, in exchange, had to accord them certain material advantages.

In the history of the relationship of Church and State under the Ptolemies, one senses, on the part of the State, the constant

desire to distinguish between gods and priests, to favor one
without necessarily ceding to the other. On the part of the
clergies, the inverse tendency, naturally, sought to triumph. If
the temple clergy had been, at the beginning of the dynasty,
proprietors of rich domains, but deprived of the right to manage
their property themselves, the priests had, in the end, obtained
power to collect the taxes themselves from the sacred land.
There is an edict given out in 118 B.C. which gives them this
right: 'No one will take by violence anything which is dedicated
to the gods, nor will torture the officers of the sacred revenues,
nor raise the taxes of association. . . nor collect the tax. . . on the
lands dedicated to the gods, nor administer, under any pretext,

Island of Philae (Description of Egypt)

the sacred *aroures*, which are to be left rather to the administration of the priests.' The king thus completely renounced his pretensions to the sacerdotal revenues as well as to the sacred land of the temples.

With the Roman conquest (30 B.C.), the relative autonomy of the clergies disappeared: all the temples of Egypt were thenceforth placed under the control of the *idiologue*, 'sovereign pontiff of Alexandria and of all Egypt,' who gave his orders to the strategists and to the other local commissioners from the central power. This regime remained until the decree by which Theodosius, in 384 A.D., ordered the closing of the temples of Egypt, officially putting an end to the old Egyptian 'paganism.'

DATE	OFFICIAL HISTORY	RELIGIOUS DATA
3000	Menes, First King.	
2800	3rd Dynasty: Djeser.	Step Pyramid of Saqqara; beginning of architecture in stone.
2700-2600	4th Dynasty: Cheops, Chephren, Mycerinus.	Pyramids and private mastabas of Giza.
2600-2400	5th Dynasty.	Little Pyramids of Saqqara; Heliopolis and the religion of the sun.
2400-2000	6th-11th Dynasties: end of Old Kingdom and 1st intermediary period.	Social revolution. Rise of the Osirian religion, of which Abydos becomes the center. Sarcophagus texts.
2000-1750	12th-14th Dynasties: the Middle Kingdom, kings Amenemhat and Sesotris.	Pyramids of the Fayoum; lake Moeris; Labyrinth; Appearance of the god Amon; vogue of the gods of the Fayoum.
1750-1580	Second intermediary period, Hyksos occupation and reconquest.	
1580	18th Dynasty: kings Amenophis and Tuthmosis.	Growth of the temporal power of Amon, god of Thebes.
1372-1343	Amenophis IV Akhenaten, Nofretete, Tut-ankh-amon.	Heresy of Amarna: exclusive cult of Aton, the sun disc.

191

DATE	OFFICIAL HISTORY	RELIGIOUS DATA
1343	General Horemheb.	Return to religious ortho-doxy.
1314-1085	19th-20th Dynasties. The Ramessides.	Vogue of the god Seth, of Re of Heliopolis and of Ptah of Memphis.
1100	The last Rameses.	Pillage of the royal tombs. Seizure of power by the Theban high priests.
	King-priests and dynasties of the Delta.	
730	Ethiopian conquest.	
663	26th Saite Dynasty; recon-quest of the country.	Sack of Thebes by the Assy-rians; vogue of the gods of the Delta, Neith, Isis, Osiris; return to ancient forms.
525	Persian conquest.	Increasing importance of the cult of sacred animals and popular magic.
400-340	28th-30th Dynasties.	Reconstruction of the tem-ples of Egypt.
341-332	Second Persian occupation.	
332	Conquest of Alexander the Great. Ptolemy kings.	Construction of the greatest temples: Edfu, Philae, Beh-beit, Esna, Medamud, Kom Ombo, Dendereh. Cult of Serapis.
30 A.D.	The Roman province of Egypt.	
384 A.D.	Theodosius.	Closing of the temples of Egypt.

ILLUSTRATIONS